Praise for *Direct Selling Success*

Top leaders agree—this book will help you build the biggest business possible!

"*I love this book!* Reading this earlier would have saved me hundreds of hours. It's the *real deal, truth*, what everybody needs to know about this business. I will be using this with my team."

—**Eugene Hong**, YOLI

"I hate this book! Because I should've written it…but it wouldn't have been this good. *Direct Selling Success* is the ultimate textbook on building a successful business."

—**Erick Gamio**

"Freaking awesome—a goldmine of information. Duplication is the key to any successful Direct Selling business and Gage is the master at teaching it."

—**Zach Bradley**, President, ZYIA Active

"I hope every Direct Selling CEO and executive reads this book!"

—**Art Jonak**, Founder, Mastermind Event

"This book is awesome! It shows you what true leadership is about, and could be written only by someone who has lived it. Our profession has never had a resource so powerful to help you reach success."

—**Dan Higginson**, Founder, Synergy Worldwide

"I could not recommend this book more and am grateful Randy wrote it. Too many books on Direct Selling have been written by people who really haven't had the success they claim or sustained success. Randy Gage has had massive success in the business and sustained it for several decades. This gives Randy insights and expertise that very few have and even fewer share."

—**Dana Collins**, Arbonne

"*Direct Selling Success* is undoubtedly the *best guide* if you are building a team! Randy gives you a clear path and, most importantly, a proven path that will help you achieve your goals. Every time I read one of his books, I feel a sense of peacefulness that reassures me that we are doing things right."

—**Lily Rosales**, FuXion Biotech

"Whether you are old school or new school, this book is for you. I love that Randy teaches how to incorporate what is new and working with the fundamental principles of Direct Selling. Through real-life experiences and his crazy, genius way of explaining things, he makes it easy to understand and duplicate."

—**Jeremiah Bradley**, CEO, Nimbus Performance

"Dream. Struggle. Victory! Wherever you are in your building process, this book will help you dream bigger, conquer your struggles, and claim your victory. You might disagree on some points. We sure did. But that will help you do the critical thinking required for your ultimate success."

—**Hilde Rismyhr Saele and Ørjan Saele**, Cofounders, Zinzino

"This is the Bible of Direct Selling! Randy's energy, passion, and scientific approach jump out at you from every chapter."

—**Jeff D. Higginson**, CEO, International FuXion Biotech

"If you are a professional networker, or just starting out in the business, this book is indispensable!"

—**Jairo Bernal**, General Manager, OMNILIFE Colombia

"I'm truly excited about this new book. If you're ready to transform your business and add digits to your income, this is the book to not just read, but reread over and over. Make sure your team does, too. People who implement the real-world truths contained within will achieve promotions and income levels that may have been beyond them otherwise. Randy Gage is the real deal."

—**Wes Linden**, member of the Direct Selling Hall of Fame and author of the bestseller *79 Network Marketing Tips*

"The immense wisdom contained in these pages—if you'll commit to taking these lessons to heart—can make you both a much more effective leader and help you rise to the highest level in your company. Really. You'll want everyone on your team (and by everyone I mean everyone serious about building a rewarding and lucrative business) to read this book, make a study of it, and, most importantly, apply its game-changing advice."

—**Bob Burg**, coauthor of *The Go-Giver* and *The Go-Giver Influencer*

"Randy wrote the ultimate guide to understanding our profession on every level. If Direct Selling was a religion, this would be its Bible."

—**Jaime Lokier**, author of *Leadership Networks* (Redes de Liderazgo)

"Randy is always thought-provoking, engaging, and interesting. His insights are not complicated rocket science but practical advice that anyone can use to build their business. I particularly like the chapter 'Leadership Landmines That Kill Growth.'"

—**Steve Critchley**, Utility Warehouse

"An amazing, amazing book. Randy Gage once again is helping us to see the future of our profession. It's not a book that's up-to-date, it's up-to-tomorrow!"

—**Dr. Hedi Khezrzadeh**, Viaveta Company

"I love this book. There are so many resources teaching techniques from 30 years ago. This is a refreshing take—the real-world, relevant, step-by-step process to be successful *today*."

—**Sam Higginson**, Former National Director of Sales, Rodan + Fields

"Simply an excellent tool for success in the business. Prospecting, presenting, building customers, enrolling, duplication, and becoming an effective leader…a recommended inclusion in your distributor kits!"

—**Sunny Ooi**, Former CEO, Malaysia ORGANO

"It's a new world in Direct Selling and this book reveals what you need to succeed in our changing profession, with proven methods and insights that will educate and inspire you to create your own global empire."

—**Lisa Jimenez, MEd,** author of *Slay the Dragon*

"Thanks to Randy's books like this one, we have managed to build organizations made of thousands of people in more than 20 countries. I highly recommend it if you are building big!"

—**Luca Melloni**, FuXion Biotech

"This business isn't rocket science, but Randy Gage will have you working your business like a NASA engineer, launching your success like an Atlas Rocket!"

—**Michael Smith**, Chief Operating Officer, Crescendo

"For both new kids and veterans, this book is Gage's current and complete nuts-and-bolts manual of how to truly succeed in this business. A proven expert in both principle and practice, Gage dissects the secrets of networking success with timely advice on using social media and building long distance. If your simple dream is to build a networking organization that thrives based on duplication, then let this book be your Bible."

—**Christopher Cooper**, Regional Director, Jeunesse Global

"Randy has done the research, experimented, and tested his theories in the business-building lab, and he knows the formula for success in this business. If there were a Nobel Prize for Direct Selling, Gage would have it. Read the book. Or spend 30 years figuring it out for yourself."

—**John Milton Fogg**, member of the Direct Selling Hall of Fame and author of *The Greatest Networker in the World*

"A brilliant roadmap for creating and breeding success in your business! Simple enough for the newbie and peppered with advanced strategies for the six- and seven-figure earner—or those who would like to be."

—**Terry Petrovick**, Founder, Happiness to Success

"Randy Gage has his finger on the pulse of the business and inspires us to be better leaders and people. Not only does he walk you through what's going wrong in your business, he shows you how to fix it in no-nonsense, easy-to-understand terms."

—**Vickie Dickson**, dōTERRA

"This is a book everyone who is serious about being successful must read. Randy shows you what it takes to achieve success in this business, the truths you need to know and apply to create leverage and duplication. Randy's experience has not only led him to have great success in this business, but he also has written a couple of seminal books about it. This is one of the most valuable to date."

—**Jorge Meléndez**, host of the *Anquiro* podcast

DIRECT SELLING SUCCESS

FROM AMWAY TO ZOMBIES

RANDY GAGE

WILEY

Library of Congress Cataloging-in-Publication Data:

Names: Gage, Randy, author.
Title: Direct selling success : from amway to zombies / Randy Gage.
Description: First Edition. | Hoboken : Wiley, 2019. | Includes index. |
  Identifiers: LCCN 2019014767 (print) | LCCN 2019015536 (ebook) | ISBN
  9781119594512 (Adobe PDF) | ISBN 9781119594567 (ePub) | ISBN 9781119594550
  (paperback) | ISBN 9781119594512 (ePDF)
Subjects: LCSH: Direct selling. | Direct marketing. | BISAC: BUSINESS &
  ECONOMICS / Marketing / Direct. | BUSINESS & ECONOMICS / Marketing /
  Multilevel. | BUSINESS & ECONOMICS / Entrepreneurship.
Classification: LCC HF5438.25 (ebook) | LCC HF5438.25 G344 2019 (print) | DDC
  658.8/72—dc23
LC record available at https://lccn.loc.gov/2019014767

Printed in the United States of America

10010993 061019

For all the people who still believe in the power of a dream...

CONTENTS

Introduction: Dream Big, Act Deliberately   *xiii*

Chapter 1   The #1 Secret for Creating Prosperity   1

Chapter 2   R.I.P. MLM   11

Chapter 3   Choosing the Right Company for You   25

Chapter 4   The Secret to Lightning-Fast Growth   63

Chapter 5   How to Construct a "Bullet-Proof"
                Duplicable System   75

Chapter 6   Building Gargantuan Customer Volume   87

Chapter 7   How to Prospect Brilliant Talent   97

Chapter 8   The Science of Successful Recruiting   119

Chapter 9   Harnessing E-Commerce and Social Media
                to Explode Growth   139

Chapter 10 Creating Sustainable Duplication and
                Profound Depth   153

Chapter 11 Building a Business the Sun Never Sets On   163

Chapter 12 Leadership Landmines That Kill Growth   173

Chapter 13 Building Your Personal Leadership Brand   187

Chapter 14 How You Become a Positive, Powerful
                Leader   197

Chapter 15 Building Belief in Your Team   209

Chapter 16   How to Create a Leadership Factory   229

Chapter 17   Becoming Wealthy, Not Just
                 "Instagram Rich"   249

Chapter 18   The Brutal Truth Nobody Else Will
                 Tell You...   257

Recommended Resources   265
"Did This Guy Write Anything Else?"   267
Acknowledgments   269
About the Author   271
Index   273

INTRODUCTION
DREAM BIG, ACT DELIBERATELY

So why did you decide to work a Direct Selling business? I mean *really?*

Was it because you wanted to become a millionaire? Earn one of those exotic supercars? Be one of those people on stage holding a six-foot-wide check with a big number on it?

Let's get real.

Personally, I joined this business to get rich. I had been broke my whole life. I hated being poor and desperately wanted to become wealthy. So that's the real-world reason I began. And there's nothing wrong if you joined for the same reason.

Just know that at some point, you're going to need something more, something better.

In my case, I was so desperate to get rich that everything I said and did was filtered through that perspective. So I looked at candidates the way wolves look at a sheep at lunchtime. Even the people I had sponsored got the vibe that my only concern was how much money they were going to make for me.

Not really a winning formula…

You've got to see candidates through a prism of how you can help them. You've got to approach the business with the mindset that if you help your team members to reach success, your own success will be assured.

I believe wealth is actually created only two ways:

1. By solving problems
2. By adding value

This is good advice to follow for your Direct Selling business. This means you have to flip the focus from you to your potential customers and team members.

For most people, their focus starts off very me-centered. You're thinking I need more customers, I need them to buy more, I've got to recruit more people, I have to find more leaders...

But that stuff is all about you. None of it is relevant to your candidates or team members.

Take a serious look at your product or service line. Ask yourself: What exactly are the benefits to my customer? Not just a general, feel-good promise like "These nutritional products will improve your health." I'm talking about specific, tangible, unique, measurable, and demonstrable benefits your customer will enjoy.

Then you want to be thinking about the benefits the business offers. These include:

- Low start-up investment
- Flexible schedule
- Travel opportunities
- Tax advantages
- Being your own boss
- Working with people you choose
- Unlimited earning potential
- Becoming successful by helping others
- No degrees or experience required

However, you must keep in mind this important point: Not all benefits matter to all people. So if you just do a "data dump" with your candidates, you won't be as successful as you could be. You'll do much better actually finding out your candidate's particular situation and what specific benefits are most compelling to her.

Here's the great news...

If you follow the advice in this book, you'll be able to weave all these important elements into a robust, successful business, doing the right things. You will be able to enjoy the monetary and recognition benefits and know that you are solving problems and creating true value.

Know that this is not a feel-good, rah-rah book. Actually, I do hope it makes you feel good about what you're doing and your ability to do it successfully. But the main purpose of this book is to be used as your textbook for becoming successful (or more successful) in the business.

You'll discover specific and tangible ways to find great candidates, qualify them, move them into a compelling series of presentations, recruit the right ones, train them, develop them, and then lead them to success.

This stuff works.

This stuff works in the real world today, even with all the changes in regulation, social media, the Internet, mobile apps, replicated websites, and economic upheaval.

In case you haven't figured it out yet, this book is the natural sequel to *How to Build a Multi-Level Money Machine*. Because the world has changed so much, I felt that instead of a new edition of the old book, it was time to start fresh, with a clean canvas.

The ever-increasing role of e-commerce, technology, and social media has impacted the business on a scale almost unimaginable even five years ago. The regulatory environment has become more complex and certainly more negative. And the public perception and portrayal of the business, which had experienced a positive swing for many years, has taken a steep slide downward.

This new book also differs from its predecessor in construction. The original book took you through the process of starting and building your business incrementally. *Direct Selling Success* is written to be a dog-eared textbook for you. It's broken down into chapters by necessary skillsets. Mark it up. Scribble notes in the margins. Fold down a page corner for quick reference. Highlight important points.

Then when you're asked to make your first presentation on stage, confronted by the idea of calling a scary candidate, or dealing with a renegade leader, you can come back to a specific chapter and get advice you can immediately apply.

Important Note: I have included five bonus chapters on high-level leadership. For you guys who are new to the business, I am strongly recommending that you initially skip Chapters 13, 14, 15, 16, and 17 (and proceed directly from Chapter 12 to Chapter 18). Those chapters are about complex leadership strategies and would probably overwhelm you if you read them now. It would be much better to come back and read them after you have been in the business at least two years.

In the chapters before them, you'll discover how to spend your time productively, develop leaders, and, most importantly, empower those leaders to develop new ones. You'll come to a clear understanding of a fundamental, profound truth about Direct Selling:

> *You don't grow your group. You grow your people—and they grow your group.*

You will find I'm not big on motivational clichés and weary, over-used platitudes. I believe that if you can show people specifically how they can accomplish a desired goal—they will motivate themselves. This book is a GPS for leading your people to success.

By the time you've finished the book, you will:

- Have a realistic view of how wealth is created in the business.
- Know the key components for developing true duplication.
- Have useful skills and strategies for prospecting and recruiting.
- Understand what top leaders do to build effectively.
- Have a specific game plan for making that happen.

Our profession is now past the 60-year mark and facing greater challenges than ever before. But with those challenges come even greater opportunities. We are going to need to reinvent ourselves. This book is my contribution to that effort.

In this business, you can earn a lot of money, win those trips to exotic locales, and drive those gorgeous bonus cars. You really do have the chance to create your freedom.

But that's the thing about freedom. It's never free…

Freedom is the byproduct of dedication, perseverance, and hard work. You must be willing to pay the price and do the work. If you are willing to do that, this book will guide you through exactly how to do it.

I didn't write the book to challenge your dreams—but rather to help you realize them. And I certainly didn't write it to change you. Instead, to help you discover and unfold into who you are really meant to be. You're about to embark on a magic carpet ride of challenge, adventure, and growth. Relish the journey.

I'm humbled and honored for your trust and accepting me as your "surrogate sponsor." Together we're going to do some great things.

Dream big, act deliberately,

—Randy Gage
Key West, Florida
January 2019

CHAPTER 1

The #1 Secret for Creating Prosperity

What is the greatest secret for creating success, wealth, and overall prosperity?

Famed Greek mathematician Archimedes best revealed that secret when he said:

> *"Give me a lever long enough and a fulcrum on which to place it, and I shall move the world."*

When he spoke those words, he was illuminating the awesome power of *leverage*. Leverage truly is the number one secret you can use to create success, develop wealth, and manifest prosperity.

The most prolific entrepreneurs on earth draw on leverage to create prosperity. Famous industrialists like John D. Rockefeller, J. Paul Getty, and Andrew Carnegie used it, as do modern-day success stories like Elon Musk, Bill Gates, and Oprah Winfrey.

With Direct Selling, everyone has the opportunity to apply leverage—just as the wealthy do—to create financial freedom and security. Every new distributor can build a solid customer base and a team of entrepreneurs—all producing residual income for themselves. Before long, your business can start spreading exponentially.

But how do you successfully build a viable Direct Selling distributorship? Allow me to share with you one of my favorite affirmations, one I use frequently:

> *I break through self-limiting beliefs and open myself to possibilities.*

The reason I use that affirmation so much is because I need it so much. Because it goes right to *the fundamental essence* of personal growth and how to become successful:

> *The need to blow up preconceived limiting beliefs we have that cause us to either lower our aspirations or even self-sabotage what we do decide to attempt.*

Once you truly understand this, your whole world changes. Because you stop looking for excuses from external sources (the economy, the Prime Minister, your ex-spouse, etc.), and you turn your attention inward.

> *No one holds you back more than you do.*

Let me suggest something you might find shocking and probably have a hard time believing. Most of the opinions, ideas, and rules you live by are lies.

They are the residue of past, limiting beliefs you haven't yet released. You were most likely programmed with those beliefs before you were 10 years old. And for you to succeed in Direct Selling, you're going to have to eradicate those beliefs. And then replace them with beliefs that actually empower you, instead of hold you back.

> *When you blow up a limiting belief like "I'm not worthy" or "I don't have the right connections/experience/education to do this," your whole world transforms in an instant.*

No, you don't get the results in an instant. You still have to make the decision, take the action, and go through the process.

But your world has explicably changed, because you're courageous enough to make that decision to start. That changes everything forward from that point.

If you're looking for reasons why something won't work, you'll never find a shortage of them. However, if you approach this business with the expectation that you're going to succeed, you dramatically improve your odds of actually doing that. Your mindset is critical—which is why I'm beginning the book with this topic.

Essentially, it's pretty simple to build a successful business in our profession. But don't confuse *simple* with *easy*. It's never easy.

There will be dropouts, no shows, and potential superstars who flame out in 30 days. You'll be competing against sleazy recruiters, Ponzi schemes, and other money games. You'll face frustration, rejection, and perhaps ridicule. And you'll face something much, much worse: your own self-doubt.

To persevere and still be here for the victory in the end, you're going to have to pay the price. Pay it gladly. Because the cost of living your dreams is high. But the cost of giving up on your dreams is much, much higher.

You're joining a business that millions of people around the globe have utilized to improve their lives. And I've seen the proof...

I've done new member orientations in Skopje, Macedonia; conducted Leadership Institutes in Zagreb, Croatia; and sponsored the first woman to ever qualify for a bonus car in Ljubljana, Slovenia.

I've seen people ride trains for 40 hours to come for training in Almaty, Kazakhstan, and show up to an event in Trujillo, Peru—via mule. I've seen the passion in the eyes of people pursuing their dreams from San Diego to London, La Paz to Sydney, Moscow to Memphis, and Seoul to a trailer park in Pensacola. Thousands have done it. Millions more are doing it.

I wrote this book to give you the best chance of replicating their success. Please think of me as your surrogate sponsor, here to guide you through the process.

Of course, this all comes back to you...

And what you do with the information you're about to receive. You're going to face challenges and face doubts. You'll be tempted to quit a hundred times.

Will you choose to be a victim or a victor?

You can't be both. You have to decide. The greatest honor you can give the force that created you is to become who you are truly meant to be. So if you're up for that, let's get after it.

WHAT YOU DON'T NEED

Before we delve into what it takes to succeed in this business at a high level, let's run through some of the things you might think you need—but actually don't.

Here's what you *don't* need to be successful in Direct Selling:

- Experience
- College degrees
- Lots of money
- Selling skills

Let's unpack each of these, and allow me to share my thoughts on each.

You Don't Need Experience

You don't need experience, because no one is going to ask you to quit your job and instantly replace your income. I'm going to recommend that you start part-time, working 10 to 15 hours a week, keeping whatever job you currently have. Just work the business as a side hustle, and see where it develops from there. You'll have no pressure, and you can learn and earn as you go along.

The real success in our business comes from duplication, employing the concept of leverage. So a lot of the time, coming in with preconceived ideas or experience can actually hold you back. Personally, I prefer to work with people who have no experience in the profession, because we don't have to go through a massive unlearning process.

You Don't Need a College Degree

Because I'm a high school dropout who became wealthy in this business, I don't think degrees and accreditations are necessary. But it's not just me. There are countless stories of successful people with no degrees. Most of the theoretical stuff they teach in business school doesn't apply here anyway.

Success in Direct Selling comes from empowering a large group of people to consistently perform a few simple behaviors on an ongoing basis. So you certainly don't need four years of higher learning to do that.

When you join a Direct Selling company, you have an entire sponsorship line that has a vested interest in your success. They will actually come down in the group to train and work with you for free. This makes having experience or a degree considerably less important than they would be in traditional businesses.

You Don't Need Lots of Money

Beginning a Direct Selling business requires a minimal investment. You don't need a physical location, employees, or a large inventory. You can start this business for literally a fraction of what traditional businesses cost to launch.

You Don't Need Selling Skills

Maybe most surprising is that you don't need selling skills. That's because no one is going to ask you to knock on the doors of strangers, make cold calls, or use high-pressure closing techniques to convince people to buy your products.

We produce literally billions of dollars (pesos, pounds, yen, rubles, and many other currencies) in sales every year. But this astounding amount of sales is created by conversationally marketing the products to friends, family, and neighbors. People you already have relationships with, who can benefit from your product or service.

You learn how to discover needs, then solve problems and add value through what you offer.

The big difference in our business is the leverage. Leverage is one of the great wonders of the world—not unlike compound interest—because it allows you to escape the trap of trading hours for money. And when you employ that leverage, following a simple, duplicable system, you might create an organization that produces literally millions of dollars in sales—even though you don't know any closing techniques or perform any of the normal behaviors you'd associate with a salesperson. This is why I call our business model *Leveraged Sales*, a concept we'll talk about more in the next chapter.

So now that you know what you don't need to be successful—what does it actually take to succeed?

What It Takes to Succeed

This business has produced some of the most remarkable and inspirational success stories you'll ever hear. Practically every company has its "rags to riches" stories of everyday people who went from poor or modest beginnings to living the lifestyle of their dreams.

From single mothers on welfare to people with disabilities, from pizza delivery drivers to the young man in Taiwan who rode his bicycle to opportunity meetings—people have rediscovered their dreams and made them happen through Direct Selling.

Across the profession, you will find striking similarities in the ultra-successful people in all companies. These common traits are the prerequisites for long-term success in the business. Let's explore exactly what the commonalities are.

Everyone in This Group Is a Dreamer

They stopped buying the gloom and doom portrayed in the media and reconnected to the vision of greatness we all once had for ourselves.

If Morpheus were to offer them the red pill or the blue pill, they would always choose the trip down the rabbit hole rather than the safety of the Matrix. Because they know that in today's world, risky is the new safe. And the people who are playing it safe are actually at the greatest risk for a life of mediocrity.

Everyone in This Group Is a Critical Thinker

They reject herd thinking and practice discernment. They are curious by nature and open to challenging their most deeply held foundational beliefs. They are not cynics, but they *are* skeptical of conventional wisdom. They question authority and want to know the reasoning behind a premise. They know any beliefs they have that serve them will survive a healthy skepticism, and any beliefs that don't stand up under scrutiny need to be replaced.

Everyone in This Group Is a Worker

They don't look for the free lunches and get-rich schemes. Far from running away from work, they get up, throw the sheets off the bed and actually look forward to work. They love challenge, growth, adventure, and helping others while helping themselves. Because they love their work so much, they don't need a 12-pack and a Netflix binge to escape from their job. They have discovered how to merge work and life into a lifestyle they love.

Everyone in This Group Is a Good Teacher

They recognize that real duplication comes from *teaching* skills much more than *selling* skills. They follow a formula that allows large numbers of people to replicate their actions.

Everyone in This Group Is Also a Student

They have a passion for lifelong learning and set aside daily time for quiet reflection and self-development.

Initially, my biggest mistake in the business was thinking that success would come from changing others. I soon learned that success comes from changing oneself. The actions you take and the examples you set create a ripple effect that impacts everything around you in a positive way. To change the world— you must first change yourself.

Everyone in This Group Is a Leader

They weren't born a leader. Nobody appointed them to the position, and they couldn't care less about titles, hierarchy, or conformity. They are called to lead from the small, still voice in their soul.

They lead because they have belief. Belief in a better way, belief in contributing to others, belief that prosperity is everyone's birthright. And they know their conviction comes with a responsibility to share that belief with the larger community.

The rules of the corporate world don't apply in Direct Selling. In this business, you get ahead not by beating out other people or holding them down, but by helping them to grow.

The more people you make successful, the more successful you become.

A corporation has room for one president, a few vice presidents, more middle managers, and then many workers at low-level jobs. In Direct Selling, we encourage everyone who desires to be a leader to strive for leadership positions. There is no limit to the number of people who can reach the top of your compensation plan.

Now that you know the attributes required to be successful in Direct Selling, let me show you why the old paradigms of Network Marketing/MLM have to die—and how we'll move forward with a better model...

CHAPTER 2

R.I.P. MLM

You want to know how the majority of network marketing companies get created? It often starts with a couple of guys, having a few (or lots of) drinks in a bar. One of them slams back a shot and says, "You know what we should do? We should start an MLM company!"

The other guy lifts his head off the bar and says, bleary-eyed, "Great idea! What should we sell?"

And then they look around and see what most other network marketing companies are selling. So they probably end up with some kind of nutrition, skin care, or cosmetics line. Next they call up a private-label company.

If they decided on nutrition, they may ask for a line with a multivitamin, energy bar, and protein shake, for example. And that private-label company will sell them the same exact multivitamin, energy bar, and protein shake they produce for a few dozen other companies. Each company has their own custom labels, but they're all selling the same mediocre crap.

These businesses weren't started to add value or solve a problem. They were created for one purpose only: to make money for the owners.

Now there's nothing morally wrong with that. But there's nothing particularly compelling about it either. And that is a recipe for what we see all too frequently in our business: *overexuberant people pitching positions in a pay plan, with no real foundation of a product that adds value.*

Overzealous product claims are a consistent, prevalent problem with most of the nutrition, wellness, and even skin care companies in our space. And we have way too many instances of ridiculous income claims made across the spectrum of companies in the business.

Then toss in the many cases of people and companies pushing recruiting at the expense of developing a viable customer base. Because this culture almost exclusively emphasizes getting new recruits, there is practically no focus on developing the customer base.

Now, if you followed my earlier work and are thinking I'm a hypocrite and you want to expose me, let me save you the time.

There's no need for you to try and uncover a scratchy audio or old, grainy video of me exhorting people that the real money was in developing the players and big recruiters. There are literally *millions* of those recordings out there, because that's what I preached for almost 20 years. So I plead guilty as charged.

I was a high school dropout who had found a way to create wealth for the first time in my life. Because I was great at team building, I naturally emphasized that in my practice and training. I felt that even if people were buying products only to get or increase a bonus check—at least they were using them and would receive the benefits. Most of us in the business felt that as long as the retailing option was available, we were fine having mostly a closed system of wholesale buyers.

But society evolves…

We used to think women shouldn't vote, leeches cured diseases, and it was acceptable to own human beings as property. As humanity evolves, our consciousness develops, and we become more enlightened.

Unfortunately, we haven't had enough of that kind of development in the more than 60-year existence of network marketing…

For at least a decade, the regulators have made clear that unless we can show a solid base of customers who are not involved in the pay plan—they're going to come after us for promoting money games, pyramids, and Ponzi schemes.

There were leaders in our space who recognized this and made changes. They created a culture where everyone who joined the team was expected to have 10, 20, or even more customers.

The generic Mastermind Event, conducted by Art Jonak and his team, has been offering extensive training on this topic for years now. I updated my training albums and developed my Academy for Network Marketing Leadership based on the principles of a large, vibrant customer base.

But we've got waaaaay too many dinosaurs left...

After the Herbalife and Vemma legal skirmishes, everybody started talking about customers. Even the cryptocurrency money games are talking about customers. But you can't just throw in the word "customers" and think you're in the clear. You have to demonstrate your legitimacy by actually having customers. And the sad truth is, many of the companies in our space don't.

They don't have them because their products are marginal, their prices are inflated, or the culture is focused on recruiting only.

We lost the plot.

We forgot that *everything* begins and ends with product volume (PV). Your company might call it customer volume (CV), qualifying volume (QV), or something similar, but the critical point is this: Every commission, override, bonus car program, and other incentive we earn has to be built on the foundation of PV.

And PV is only the volume produced by products actually purchased and used by the end consumer.

It's time to regain the plot.

The business model known as MLM—multi-level or network marketing—is facing serious and I believe insurmountable threats. We've snatched defeat from the jaws of victory.

We took this amazing business model—arguably the last bastion left in the free enterprise system, where an average, ordinary person can create extraordinary wealth and success—and perverted it. Hustlers, con artists, and greedy opportunists have hijacked it.

We need to initiate a bold, daring, and creative dialogue about the future—and what we can do to create a better one for the millions of people impacted by what we do. In 2017 I wrote a manifesto about this. Now this book is the next step.

If you are up for helping our profession to move forward to the next generation of development and want to be part of the movement to make that happen—then by all means, keep reading.

But first we must acknowledge the fact that this business model—which so many of us love, which has created prosperity for millions—is dying. The cancer has spread too far, too fast. And we let it happen. Time to put it out of its misery.

R.I.P. MLM

So where do we go from here? How do we rid ourselves of the charlatans who have taken over the business and turned it into a cesspool? How do we repair the damage they've caused and restore the reputation of network or multi-level marketing?

The sad answer is, we don't. The swindlers, con artists, and criminals have destroyed the good reputation of the business and we're never going to get it back. Instead of hoping something happens to change our story, we need the courage to change it ourselves.

I believe the most liberating day of your life will be the one in which you realize that some bridges are meant to be burned. And this tired and misconstrued model known as multi-level marketing needs to be burned.

MLM is dead. It's time to place the wreath on the coffin and lower it into the ground.

But getting products and services to people who love them is still very much alive. It's time to reinvent the way we do that.

We need a fresh start...

I realize that a growing number of the reputable companies remaining have been using new terms like network sales, affiliate marketing, or Direct Selling. I don't think any of those labels really capture the most exciting part of our business, which is leverage.

So all I can do is share with you what I'm doing personally...

I have stopped using the labels like MLM, multi-level, or network marketing. For all marketing and training materials, and all recruiting presentations moving forward, I've already started transitioning to a new name: Leveraged Sales.

LEVERAGED SALES

Leveraged Sales captures the true essence of what made the business great to begin with. These two interlocked elements essentially define what we do:

> *Create sales and then employ the concept of leverage to exponentially increase the rewards for those people producing those sales.*

We can employ innovative strategies and new technologies, like enticing preferred customer programs, convenient autoship options, easy customer interface for online sales, and expedient mobile app ordering. And we can integrate the concept of leverage, which, like compound interest, is one of the true wonders of the world.

But this time around, we must work tirelessly, vigilantly, and relentlessly to keep out the people who try to use our legitimate structure as a cover to exploit others.

The governments are always a step behind the perpetrators. With new technology like blockchains and cryptocurrencies, the gap is even larger. There are too many people with bad intentions and not enough regulators to police them.

We have to regulate ourselves.

We don't have to tear down other companies to make our own look better. That's poverty consciousness and actually hurts us all. When a competitor does a better job than you, tip your cap to them and resolve to be better next time. *But we have to stop looking the other way when we see people and companies operating unethically.* We need to speak up when we see questionable practices, sham products, and recruiting deception.

We have to expose the corrupt leaders and companies that are practicing these deplorable activities. And keep them out of our new space.

We're going to have to change the rules, change the game, and, most importantly, change the results. We have to go old school—driven by principles and operating with integrity. We're going to reinvent the best model in the free enterprise system for the ordinary person to create extraordinary results.

After all, we were the original disrupters in the marketing space. Now we're going to disrupt it again.

It's not going to be easy…

In fact, it's going to be extremely difficult. It will take years to accomplish. And we'll face resistance at every step of the way.

Billions of dollars in sales in the old recruit-first model will be threatened. Change scares people. Some will be frightened and will lash out at us.

Money games and pyramid schemes also generate billions of dollars in revenue. There are thousands of people vested in these corrupt programs. They won't go quietly or easily.

Both the media and the general public are going to be skeptical of us, question our motives, and doubt our sincerity. It's going to take the dedicated commitment of a core group of people who want to be agents of change. People who believe in the real mission: empowering entrepreneurs to build lucrative customer bases.

If you're up for the challenge, willing to leave the past behind, and ready to evolve into the next generation of what we do—then I invite you to join me in this next adventure.

Let's look at some of the things we're going to have to do better or do differently.

1. If You Want to Build a Leveraged Sales Business, You Have to Sell

As I told you in Chapter 1, you don't have to master closing techniques, knock on the doors of strangers, or make cold calls. You don't have to hype products or manipulate people either. You just have to be a great ambassador for products or services you fervently believe in. If you're not willing to do that, quit now. This new business model isn't for you.

Leveraged Sales is for people who passionately believe in the product or service line they represent, and they want to tell others about those products or services.

You may worry that this strategy will limit the people who enter the business. That's not really a problem. You're going to encounter people who say they don't want to sell. Great. They shouldn't join the business to begin with.

2. Stop Being so Gullible

The reason money games and get-rich-quick schemes work is they prey on people's greed. So many people today are looking for a "hack" that eliminates the work required for success. There is no such thing as an "automated down-line building system," and there never will be. Stop looking.

3. Protect Yourself and Your Team Against the Cottage Industry of Parasites that Latch Onto Our Profession to Make Money Off Of You

There are trainers, consultants, and coaches who don't know the first thing about our profession, but they create huge businesses selling advice to us. Most of them don't produce anything or offer any real value. So they will certainly follow us to our new destination.

They may claim to be amazing recruiters, brilliant sales coaches, or social media savants. Use a little common sense. If they really had the secret for success in our business, they'd be doing it themselves.

And in the new business environment today, we now have to deal with all the distractions of the online world. You also have to inoculate your team against the review, watchdog, and industry news websites.

The people who run these sites are experts at SEO marketing, so they always come up near the top of the results when people search company names. Ninety-five percent of these are detrimental to your business. You have to practice *discernment*.

Some of these sites are well-meaning but misguided. Some are designed solely as "bait and switch"—meaning they lure you to read a review on your company, but it's actually a hit piece designed to switch you over to their company.

Some conduct polls for best trainer, CEO, or company. The real purpose of these surveys is to capture the emails of your team members so they can recruit them or sell them crap.

There's a guy out there promoting a site with huge reach that is simply a PR platform. He gets paid a monthly retainer to write nice things about his clients each month. And when they stop paying him, he writes horrible things about them.

Don't allow yourself to be manipulated. These sites matter only to the "MLM Zombies" who don't know any better. Stay away from them and keep your people off their mailing lists.

You also need discernment for the newspapers, newsletters, and magazines that cover our profession. Most are just like the websites I mentioned. People *buy* placement as a "rising star" or featured profile. If you're willing to shell out $25K, you can even be an international cover model. 🤢

So here's how the system works now…

The scummiest and most questionable schemes eagerly pay to have their programs and top leaders featured. Then they use reprints of these articles to appear legitimate in order to lure in more unsuspecting victims.

Again the key word here is discernment. Be discerning about every guru, coach, consultant, author, website, and publication. Including this book.

4. Stop Trying to Compete with the Bad Guys

You can't. And you don't want to. A bank robber can take down as much money in 20 minutes as a plumber earns in 20 years. That doesn't mean you should rob banks.

Yes there will be people claiming they made $10,000 or $20,000 their first month in some deal or another. That may be true if they rolled over a team from another scheme and have a special arrangement with a "cooked leg." (This means a special arrangement where one or more lines are auto-qualified.) Don't try and match that; you can't. The candidates they're attracting with those hype pitches are not the people you're looking for anyway.

5. Stop Promoting Five- and Six-figure Monthly Incomes

For decades now, when you started building a network marketing presentation, the first thing you did was grab photos of a Lamborghini, sandy beaches, and stacks of cash. Then you trotted out those five- and six-figure monthly earners. But the world has changed. We have to leave the propaganda behind. Practically speaking, these tropes aren't nearly as effective as they used to be anyway.

Companies that recruit on examples of five- and six-figure monthly incomes are going to get killed by the regulators. It doesn't matter how many fine-print disclaimers you use. Those kinds of results are not typical and they never will be. *If you make these kinds of claims, you are going to get shut down.*

The truth is, we do have many people that make outrageous amounts of money. Make no mistake—any income above $25,000 a month is perceived as outrageous by almost any standard. The vast majority of people can't relate to earning that kind of money. They would be *delighted* to have a side hustle that produced $800 a month in residual income. They would be OVER THE MOON to have a part-time business that provided them with $3,000 a month in residual income.

There are at least six (and maybe seven) billion people on earth whose lives would be dramatically and measurably impacted if you could simply help them earn an extra couple hundred dollars (or the equivalent in their currency) a month to meet their basic needs.

Their lives would be dramatically and measurably impacted in a meaningful way if you could simply help them get out of debt. And talking about getting out of debt is a lot sexier than you may think. It resonates with people. Even people who are not in debt have parents, siblings, and friends who are upside down in their car payments, have oppressive mortgages, and are suffocating in student loans and credit card debt. Stop hyping extreme incomes and start offering people a pathway to get out of debt, and you'll do a lot better.

6. Stop Job-shaming, Education-shaming, and Promoting to the Lowest Common Denominator

We have to stop denigrating college, acting like all bosses are evil, or that everyone with a job is a loser. Here's a revolutionary idea…

Let's start with the premise that most people don't appreciate being patronized, ridiculed, or looked down upon.

If you want to help them, stop judging them. If you want them to join your business, begin the process by treating them with respect. Suggesting they're an idiot for going to college, or a loser because they have a job, is probably not the best way to inspire someone to join your business.

The reality is that many people have good educations and enjoy their jobs. Or maybe they earn a lot of money with their job, but it doesn't offer the freedom and lifestyle choices they are looking for. Or just maybe, they love their job and want to keep it, but it doesn't pay them very well. Let's be open to all possibilities and meet people where they are.

You don't have to be sleeping under a bridge to join Leveraged Sales. We have to kill the meme that everyone who is successful in our business used to be destitute, homeless, or bankrupt.

Don't get me wrong: If you are poor, facing challenges, or struggling with personal issues—this business offers you a way to become the next success story. We'll celebrate that. And we all love to hear those redemption stories from the stage. But not everyone is staring down a disastrous calamity and in desperate need of rescue.

We need to make the business attractive to people at all different levels of success in their lives. So we also need to celebrate the people with good educations, high-paying jobs, and solid financial situations who choose to enter our business.

Recruiting isn't about fitting people into the slots you have. It's about offering them avenues to achieve what they desire.

When I'm asked to present the Leveraged Sales business these days, you know what I talk about?

Building a solid customer base. Creating a residual income to enhance what your dream lifestyle looks like. And getting "the money thing" out of the way.

No six-foot-wide checks on the stage. No Lambos. No mention of high monthly incomes. Just a simple conversation about getting out of debt and designing your dream life.

It works. And it will work for you—if you let it.

We can be successful without the embellishment, the questionable tactics, and the deceit. There's a whole world of people out there looking for products and services that can make their lives better. And scores of people who not only have a desire to create a residual income—but they are actually willing to work for it.

Which is the other reason I'm publishing this book…

I recognize that many of the people currently working in the old model of hype and rah-rah are actually good folks. I have friends in this category. Friends who I know would have never knowingly joined anything that was unethical or would hurt people.

They're ignorant about developing tech like blockchains or don't understand the distinction between selling a product versus an investment. Someone they trusted convinced them that the tactics they use are ethical and legal, and they unwittingly suspended their judgment and went along with them. They're simply not knowledgeable enough to understand they are scamming people and being scammed themselves.

I'm hoping we can rescue some of those people and bring them back from the dark side...

Working together, we can build the new business model and empower some very deserving people. We can make money, have fun, and still make the world a better place than when we found it. Yes, MLM is dead. But we don't need to be sad at the funeral. We can celebrate the good memories it provided us, apply the lessons we learned, and evolve to the next level of entrepreneurship and empowerment.

If you're still with me, and committed to reinventing the profession, let's explore how you select the right company for you...

0

0

0

<CHAPTER 3>

CHAPTER 3

Choosing the Right Company for You

One of the most important decisions you will make in your Direct Selling career is which program you choose to build with. Unfortunately, most people spend less time evaluating which companies to work with than they do choosing a data plan for their cell phone. In fact, most people let the company select them. You'll probably end up in a better place if you do a little research before you just jump into a company.

Now, for most of you reading this book, you've already done your evaluation and have found a company you're already working with. If so, feel free to skip over this chapter. You won't hurt my feelings, I promise. It's here for those who are exploring the idea of the business and haven't found a home yet. Or maybe something dramatic happened and you had to leave your last company and are now looking for a good fit. If so, then this chapter is for you. Let's begin by clarifying the difference between...

ILLEGAL PYRAMIDS VERSUS LEGITIMATE PAY PLANS

Because of the increased regulation in our space, great care should be taken on staying out of legal challenges. So let's take a quick snapshot of four criteria for separating legitimate override compensation plans from the illegal pyramids and money games. (Laws are different all around the world. But these four guidelines are good general practices to follow everywhere.)

1. Substantial Sales of Products or Services to Ultimate Users

The key here is that the products are reaching the end consumers. If someone asks you to buy $20,000 worth of wrist heart monitors to qualify for a bonus or rank advancement, it's obvious you're not going to be the end user of all those. You've been "front-loaded" (sold much more inventory than you can resell in a reasonable time) and this is not a legitimate program.

Here's the other issue in this area...

A lot of your product consumption will likely come from distributors, meaning people who enjoy the products, but also do the business and qualify to receive overrides and commissions. That produces strong volume but will present an issue when you are facing scrutiny from regulators.

Some people joined the business, didn't really have any success, but they've stayed in the system to get discounts on the products. Or sometimes people join as distributors just to purchase wholesale. You probably view them as customers. Regulators still view them as distributors. And one of the standards being propagated by regulators now is that a company must have at least 51 percent of their people ordering regularly as customers. And the regulators' definition of this means nondistributors, people who never are qualified to earn commissions.

So having customers register as a distributor to purchase at wholesale or reduced prices can present serious legal issues for companies today. Increasingly, regulators are making the case that these people are not customers, but unsuccessful victimized distributors. And they are using them as an argument that the business opportunity isn't valid.

So it's very important that there be a real difference between being a customer and a distributor. For example, a free signup to register as a distributor is actually a very bad idea. Because then there really is no reason why every customer wouldn't sign up as a distributor just to get the wholesale price. And this could end up as a regulatory nightmare down the road.

Some companies are pursuing a different but also effective approach. They don't offer a wholesale price. Distributors and customers pay the same price. And in some cases, customers are the only ones who receive free shipping and some other perks. This encourages people who want only to buy product—but not build the business—to be a happy customer, not a "distributor customer."

Then the distributors earn on their customers' orders directly through the pay plan. Only those distributors in the plan can qualify for these overrides and commissions. So the end result is the desired one, a clear distinction between customers and distributors.

2. Commissions Should Be Paid Only on Product Volume, Never on "Headhunter" Fees

Your income must come from bonuses and overrides based on the product volume produced by your team. By this I mean the volume produced by products or services actually paid for and received by the customers. If you're paid simply for signing up someone—then you're probably in a pyramid.

Very few companies will advertise that you actually make your money from signups. But you have to use your common sense, because there are a lot of sketchy deals that in essence actually do this. They have created special enrollment packages for new recruits with large overrides for the recruiter. A quick overview of company sales reveals that the vast majority of their sales, and the leaders' income, come from those packages alone. These companies count on a high turnover rate to fuel hype. But eventually they die off, because there is little ongoing product usage.

3. Make Money from the Mine, Not the Miners

The profession has a long and troubled history of cases where high-ranking distributors in programs are making a large percentage of their income from the sale of business-building materials and training. This is illegal in many markets and a questionable practice in all of them.

*The business opportunity, by itself, needs to be a **viable** business opportunity.*

If a distributor has to charge money to train his team, there's a problem. If he is making money off the sales of the marketing materials the team uses to build their business—that creates an inherent conflict of interest.

This doesn't mean everyone who does this is doing so with nefarious intent. Sometimes these tools produced by the team are the most effective ones, superior to what the company could produce. But the conflict is still there.

One of the results of this practice is people touting their incomes at a certain rank, but not disclosing that a large percentage or even a majority of their income is from training or tool sales outside of the compensation plan and not available to most distributors. This practice is unethical.

Other times these deals are camouflaged as legitimate product offerings. A perfect example is the "be a travel agent" deals that were all the rage in the 1990s. These pseudo travel agents faced much-deserved legal challenges. That's because if you looked at the numbers, most of their sales and commissions came from selling their marketing websites to the distributors themselves. They weren't coming from selling travel, which allegedly was the product.

4. Inventory Repurchase Requirements

Most of the states and provinces with relevant statutes about our business require companies to repurchase inventory that is returned by their distributors. These states also require this policy to be stipulated in the distributor agreement.

In most cases, this buy-back requirement becomes effective only when the distributor terminates his or her distributorship. In other cases, the company must repurchase any returned inventory simply if the distributor was unable to resell it within 90 days from buying it. (In both cases, there are some specifics. Usually, the buy-back is for 90 percent of the purchase price; the products must be resalable; and any commissions paid on the sold products may be deducted.)

Companies that comply with these four criteria are in line with both the letter and the spirit of the law. But we're not done yet...

OTHER QUESTIONABLE CLUBS

Another area I need to address is the "gifting" clubs. Their whole argument is that they don't need products, because the participants in the program voluntarily give gifts of money to the sponsorship line. Gifting programs are nothing more than knockoffs of chain letters, and they are illegal virtually everywhere.

And how many times will people keep trying to bring back the discount clubs, flogging products or services that are of questionable value? These have been tried again and again and never worked. The marketplace doesn't support them, and regulators slam them, because the discounts they promote are no more valuable than those available to anyone who simply shops around or are members of different associations.

The product or service must be a legitimate one that people would buy at the retail price on the open market.

If almost no one would likely buy the product or service without participating in the compensation plan, you are probably looking at a pyramid. If you are counting on the lure of the business opportunity to so excite your candidate that he will not notice he is overpaying for your product, you will be greatly disappointed. A strong retail base of happy customers (who are not in it for the bonus checks) is one of the best indicators of a strong company.

Another variation of this to beware of is the "buyer's clubs." These programs advertise that there is no selling required and suggest you are simply signing up everyone to buy wholesale. Most governments take a very dim view of such closed marketing systems, considering them pyramids. Here's why:

You can start a wholesale club, just like Sam Walton did, and it's perfectly legal. But take a wholesale club and put a multi-tiered commission structure on it—then that "club" becomes illegal in most cases, because it's a closed system. Since everyone is a member, there's no one to sell to. If all we had to do was shop to earn, everybody would be doing it. It's not that simple. So stay away from these.

FINDING THE RIGHT FIT

Okay, once you know the program you're looking at isn't illegal, how do you make sure it's a good fit for you? I said above that most people let the company pick them. There are two schools of thought on this.

First perspective: If you're presented an opportunity by someone you know and trust—and they'd like to sponsor you and are committed to working with you—there's a good deal of power in that. It's not necessary for you to go out and research every other Direct Selling company in the profession and do a side-by-side comparison. You would spend two years on research—and about the time you should be receiving some decent income, you'd be just getting started instead.

Second perspective: The company you join does play a dramatic role in your chances for success. At the very least, you need to do enough due diligence to select a good one. This is the camp I'm in.

So how do you do that? Well, I *don't* want you taking two years to research and evaluate every possible opportunity. But you can certainly ask some intelligent questions and perform due diligence on the company you are considering. So start with…

The Product. The Product. The Product.

You can begin your product line evaluation with two disqualifying questions. If the answer isn't a resounding yes to both, you should eliminate that company and keep looking.

This will facilitate your evaluation process greatly, because these two questions will likely eliminate about 98 percent of the programs you look at.

The two essential questions are:

1. If you were not participating in the business opportunity, would you buy this product or service anyway?

2. Would you buy that product or service *at that price?*

Be honest with yourself. If the answer is no, find another company. If the opportunity you're involved with is not centered on products you believe in and will personally use—it is highly unlikely that you will be successful with this company. Direct Selling is driven by the genuine enthusiasm and personal testimonials of the people involved.

Two of the first things your candidates will ask are:

1. Are the products are any good?

2. Do you use them yourself?

If you can't answer with an enthusiastic yes to both questions, they are not likely to get involved with you.

If you wouldn't pay the price for your products on the open market, it's unlikely anyone else will. Don't think people will pay more for a product simply because they might get a bonus check. It's been shown time and time again they won't.

Your success will be based on getting your products to the end consumers who actually use them and reorder them often. People who buy products just to get a bonus check end up stockpiling them and will eventually stop buying when their garage is full or their credit card is maxed out.

> *You need to have customers who are willing to pay the normal retail price for your products. This doesn't mean your company must sell products at a lower cost than what's available somewhere else. It means that your products must be of such value that you and other people are willing to pay the price for them.*

In fact, many Direct Selling companies have products that cost more than similar products available elsewhere. But due to their high quality, effectiveness, or concentration, they actually offer better value to the consumer.

We've introduced a large number of products to the general public that would never have stood a chance in the traditional distribution system. These products have helped millions of people and, arguably, even saved and extended lives.

Direct Selling companies were promoting many breakthrough health products, concentrated products, and planet-friendly packaging decades before these ideas reached popular consciousness. We also led the field with more all-natural and non-GMO products long before they were trendy.

Of course, the other tangible advantage is the personalized service and attention a customer receives from you. Customers are willing to pay a little more for this one-on-one effort from you. So don't worry if you don't have the cheapest product on the market. *What really matters is whether you're offering a suitable value.*

Let's look at the other product variables you should be considering as you evaluate a company.

The Most Marketable Product Lines Are Unique, Exclusive, and Highly Consumable

Ideally, you want products that are available exclusively from your company so your customers can get them only from you. If products just like yours are for sale in numerous retail stores and websites, you're likely to face more challenges unless your price point is dramatically lower. And selling on lower price is always a race to the bottom that you can't win.

Consumable products like nutrition, skin care, personal care, utilities, and cleaning products work better longterm than non-consumables like water purifiers, air filters, or jewelry. I know our business is filled with nutrition, household products, and personal care companies, but there's a reason for that: They work.

If your people use up shampoo, laundry soap, or vitamins on a continuous basis (as most civilized people do), you're likely to experience more frequent orders. Likewise for utility programs, because people are using their Internet, electricity, heating oil, or cell phone continuously. This means higher volumes and bigger residual bonus checks for you.

The problem is many companies want to stand out, and they take the "unique and exclusive" concept too far. In recent years there have been an avalanche of companies launching with very nontraditional product lines, such as cryptocurrencies, foreign exchange networks, and ridesharing apps. Someone approached me recently with a program built around a $6,000 medical device—a one-time purchase for medical centers. These programs fail to take into account a basic truth: Some products are great—but they're not great for a Direct Selling pay plan. (And, of course, some products aren't great in either context.)

The Problem with Cryptocurrencies for Direct Selling

As someone who leans Libertarian and chafes at the government meddling in and controlling my personal life, I'm intrigued by the whole idea of cryptocurrencies. In fact, readers of mine will know that I predicted their emergence years ago in my book *Risky Is the New Safe*.

My favor toward them is based on my skepticism to trust the viability of any government currency. After all, government budgets are the biggest Ponzi schemes the world has ever known. Currencies like the dollar, peso, and pound do not hold any intrinsic value; they are simply promises to pay. They can be valued and devalued at the whims of a government bureaucrat. (And constantly are.)

So regarding the concept of cryptocurrencies, I'm a big fan. They have the potential to facilitate secure, authenticated transactions between a buyer and seller without the intervention of a bank or a government.

But to start a Direct Selling company around a cryptocurrency as the product line is simply a preposterous idea.

It would be like starting a company and announcing that the product line was the US dollar or the Japanese yen. What would be the business proposal?

"Buy this $20 bill for $27 and maybe next year it will be worth $30."

Whether we use bitcoin, the US dollar, or the British pound (or any other currency), none of these things is a value-producing asset. They don't generate earnings or pay dividends. They are simply a trading play. You can bet they go up or bet they go down.

People who invest in a cryptocurrency today are betting it is going to rise in value. They're not likely to use it to purchase anything. So it's not really acting as a currency but an investment vehicle. You can make the argument that you are a currency trader. But that's not what we're discussing here. Cryptocurrencies can be traded or invested in—and someday soon will be used frequently to actually pay for things—but they are certainly not a viable product line for a Direct Selling company.

So how do these companies claim to be viable network opportunities? That's where ICOs come in...

Initial Coin Offerings (ICOs)

ICOs (initial coin offerings) are the cryptocurrency equivalent of a stock market IPO. And just as much of a crapshoot. (Actually, probably a lot more.) Here's how they work.

Usually an ICO involves a company raising money by selling a new digital currency. If you buy it, you receive a "token" to which they assign a value. But unlike an IPO in the stock market, the token does not give you any ownership rights in the company or entitle you to any sort of dividends.

If that cryptocurrency succeeds and appreciates in value—completely and totally based on speculation—you make a profit. But remember, there are absolutely no regulations or safeguards on this. The company that issues the tokens can often manipulate the value in a way that benefits them.

What do governments think about ICOs? Not much. They are eyeing them with wariness in some cases and outlawing them in others. Personally, I believe ICOs will be the biggest area of fraud and victimization in the business world over the next couple years. They are ripe for abuse.

They are the perfect petri dish for development of the "greater fool theory." (The premise of the theory is that the price of an object is determined not by any intrinsic value, but instead by irrational beliefs and expectations of market participants. A price can be justified by a rational buyer under the belief that another party is willing to pay an even higher price.)

And these new scams are making the most of this ignorant and irrational greed...

The scary part is these are getting more sophisticated each time. The original scam never published a white paper or actually offered an ICO. It's doubtful if they really had a blockchain.

But these subsequent scams have built on the duplicity of the original and are taking the hype even higher. They've learned all the right buzzwords and woven them into the marketing pitches.

One I saw published a "roadmap," starting with their ICO, and then making projections of what the value of their token would be at each stage of their anticipated product development. It's just sophisticated enough to fool the semi-educated dot-com billionaire wannabes (wanting to get rich without doing any actual, you know, work) who fall for this sort of hype.

As if that were not bad enough, this cryptocurrency hype is now bringing back the Forex schemes…

I won't waste much time on these, other than to say they're currently enjoying a dead cat bounce. The crypto craze has breathed new life into a concept that has already been proven to be a horrible model for Direct Selling.

If you want to become an investor, or day trader, in currencies or cryptocurrencies, wonderful. Best of luck, and have a great life. But don't be foolish enough to think that they are a viable product for a Direct Selling pay plan. They're not.

The Product Is Viable

Chairs are great products. Whenever I want to sit down, I look for the nearest chair. Tires are a great product. Whenever I buy a car, I always check to see if it comes with tires. But chairs and tires are terrible products for a Direct Selling pay plan.

At the time I'm writing this, I have two people on Facebook telling me what a moron I am, because I'm not signing up for their new program built around a ridesharing mobile app. They think I don't understand the potential of mobile and ridesharing. (Just shows they haven't done their homework, because ridesharing apps were another trend I predicted in my *Risky* book.)

I know the potential, the risks, and the rewards better than they do. *And* I understand what types of characteristics make the best products for Direct Selling.

In the plan they showed me, there are no actual commissions on the trips the drivers make. The pay plan is based entirely on the concept of *getting people to pay $2,400 for the right to become a driver,* then there are one-time commissions on that fee. Which begets a lot of questions…

It's hard enough to get three people to pay a $50 registration fee and become a distributor to market vitamins, cosmetics, or whatever. How much more difficult will it be to get three people to pay $2,400? Will regulators see this as a headhunter fee and declare the program illegal? Can this company really compete against entrenched competitors who have billions of dollars in cash and have shown a willingness to lose money for years in an attempt to drive competitors out of market after market? Lots of probing questions we could ask, right?

But none of them even matter when we get to the basic one, which is the viability of the product line.

They are building their whole company on the premise that they have a superior product to Uber and will steal the market share from them. But here's the problem with that logic. In my opinion, *the Uber model isn't even viable.* (And I believe Uber is and was aware of this from the get-go.)

It is not cost effective to have all the drivers and cars needed for peak times, and then absorb all those costs during off times, which is 70 percent of the time. Uber works only in the long term—when it can eliminate their drivers, have a totally autonomous fleet, and use that fleet for other uses (like package delivery) during nonpeak hours. So the very thing this startup is modeling the commission plan on—drivers paying a fee to drive—is the element that I believe Uber will need to eliminate to be profitable.

Let's look at the example of the medical device I mentioned earlier…

It might be the greatest medical invention since the x-ray. (And maybe it is.) But a product that only licensed medical professionals can use is certainly not going to provide ongoing consumption. And a $6,000 price tag is never going to create duplication. So the product might be great. It could be very lucrative for a salesperson to sell and profitable for the company that makes it. (And probably is.) But it's not a good product for a Direct Selling model.

It's not my goal to pick on these companies. I hope they end up becoming great successes. I just don't believe they'll be Direct Selling success stories, because the product doesn't meet the criteria. I'm beating this to death because it's vital that you understand everything starts and ends with the viability of the product line.

If the product concept isn't viable, the funding, corporate team, logo design, celebrity endorsers, or compensation plan are entirely irrelevant.

Other Desirable Qualities

Okay, we've established that the products that work best are unique, exclusive, and highly consumable. What are some other qualities you look for?

Are the product's benefits demonstrable? Can your stain remover take spaghetti sauce off a white blouse? Do people quickly see the pounds drop off when they use your weight loss product? Can they quickly feel the jolt from your energy drink?

Do the products create an emotional connection? When people actually do lose weight, clear up their acne, or save money, this creates a feel-good connection with the product line.

Are your products in front of any trends? If they're all-natural, organic, or good for the planet—these are the kinds of rising trends customers want to be associated with.

What kind of monthly volumes are likely to be produced by the products you market? The higher the monthly average is, the bigger your profit potential will be.

Suppose you're in a company with only one product, an energy drink that sells for $30 and the average person uses one bottle a month. With 100 distributors and customers in your organization, you would get paid on a volume of $3,000.

Now suppose you're in a company with an energy drink, meal replacement bars, a multi-vitamin, antioxidants, and fiber caplets. (Or a skincare company with moisturizing cream, lip balm, toner, anti-wrinkle gel, and sunblock. Or a home products company with window cleaner, wood polish, tile cleaner, soap, and floor wax.) Say the average monthly volume per family is $100. With the same 100 distributors and customers, you would be receiving override commissions on a volume of $10,000.

All other things being equal, you're going to make more money in a multiple-products company than a single-product one. Of course, this means you make more retail profits as well.

This doesn't mean you can't make money in a one-product company. If the product has a high-dollar monthly cost, or if people need to buy it a lot during a month, you'll produce and get paid on higher volumes. But here's the bottom line: *The higher the average monthly product usage, the greater your profit potential will be.*

These product questions are the foremost considerations you should have as you choose a company. Real, long-term organizational growth is driven by product demand. The compensation plan, company leadership, and other factors are all secondary to the product.

There are opportunists and even some trainers out there who will tell you that the products don't matter. They insist that the compensation plan is what drives growth. This may be true initially (when the hype machine is in full swing), but you cannot sustain your business longterm if your products are not a value to the consumer.

If people view products simply as a means to get a bonus check, they don't really use them. They don't develop the emotional bond so critical to long-term success.

It is this emotional connection to your company's products that motivates people to grow and also keeps them from jumping to the next hot deal that comes along.

Okay, let's assume that all of the product criteria are met. What are the other factors important in selecting the right company for you?

Your Sponsor and Sponsorship Line

Arguably, the next most important item to consider is your sponsor and sponsorship line. Select them as you would if you were choosing business partners to invest a million dollars in a franchise.

They are going to be your coaches and your support structure, and you're going to be spending a lot of time with them in the next two to four years. And beyond that—hopefully—a few decades together, taking cruises, drinking from coconuts, and frolicking at resorts around the world.

There is a pervasive belief that if you are a moral person, you are compelled to sign up under whoever sold you that first bottle of product or first mentioned the name of the company to you. That makes as much sense as saying you are morally obligated to build your Pizza Hut franchise on the first vacant property you see, even if it is out in the country. This is a serious choice that you should make mindfully.

It's important that your sponsor be someone you like, trust, and would enjoy working with. Don't think you must sponsor in with someone who's making a big check or is a "heavy hitter." The qualities above are much more important. In fact, in cases of rapid growth...your best sponsor might be someone who's not yet making $50 a month.

This is because in an organization that is growing fast (the kind you want to be in), it's not unusual for it to go down four or five levels in depth in a single month. These new people don't yet have experience or big checks, but they might have the drive, vision, and enthusiasm necessary to build an organization.

However, you do want to make sure there is some experience at the top of the organization somewhere. You want someone who has already successfully done what you are looking to do.

If you're going to fly to Hawaii from California, you're better off doing it with a pilot who has actually flown a real plane, not just computer simulations.

Note: Just because a candidate should be mindful of whom she chooses as her sponsor, that doesn't mean it's "open season" on stealing candidates from other distributors. If you notice that Jenny brought a candidate named Jeremy to an event, you shouldn't be trying to poach Jeremy. That's unethical. And just tacky.

Look for a sponsorship line that has a step-by-step system in place. The system should include the recruiting process, product training, "get started" training, and live events (online and offline) for ongoing training.

This information should be specifically spelled out and available to everyone in the organization. It should explain what action to take and what materials to use at each step of the recruiting and sponsoring process.

This is important to you for two reasons:

First, it will greatly speed up the time it takes you to build your group. By having a system that outlines exactly what to do, you won't waste valuable time wondering what to do next or pursuing strategies that don't work. Such a system includes only the methods and techniques that have proven themselves and stood the test of time.

The second reason a system is so important is that it ensures the people you introduce into the business will be able to duplicate your success. Their education level or their business experience ceases to be an issue. They simply follow the system exactly as you (and your sponsorship line) did.

EXAMINING THE COMPANY

Finally, after all these other factors, you can start to look at the non-product specifics of the company...

Startup Versus Established Company

One of the frequent questions I receive is whether it's better to join a startup or a mature company. Both types have advantages, so you want to choose based on what's most important to you. I worked with established companies and had moderate success. I joined two start-up companies on the ground floor only to find out later there was a basement! But I also joined a company about six months after launch that went on to become a serious player, made me millions of dollars, and in which I was able to create a legacy position for myself. Which option is right for you depends a lot on your personality.

The truth is, most new Direct Selling companies will go out of business within two years. Of course, it's also true that most new restaurants, dry cleaners, and dog grooming companies will go out of business within two years. That's the nature of business in the entrepreneurial system—90 percent of startups fail. Direct Selling is no better and no worse. So, does that mean you should avoid startups? Maybe.

It's true that the odds a start-up company will fail are greater than those of a 10-year-old established one. Yet there is a certain allure to start-up companies, a chance to "get in on the ground floor"—that attracts people. If the company has a bonus pool for founders, or similar-type program, you could get in early and qualify for very lucrative income streams that will not be available in later years.

And not incidentally, how many massive, established, even 100-year-old companies have vanished in recent years, because they didn't adapt to the changing economy?

Woolworth's, Blockbuster Video, Toys "R" Us, Lehman Brothers, Kodak, anyone?

A company that's new and not yet known has tremendous growth potential. You have the possibility of greater risk, but also the corresponding opportunity for greater rewards.

On the other hand, working with a household name gives you a certain amount of credibility to begin with, and you're likely to face less skepticism.

If you're not adverse to a certain degree of risk, you may enjoy the challenges of a start-up opportunity and the chance to cash in big-time as you ride a new company to the top. If you're more conservative and looking for greater security, go with an established company. Choose the situation that best matches your personality, needs, and financial objectives.

Debt, Cash, and the Company's Capital

Another standard you'll hear mentioned frequently is whether the company is debt-free. Truth is, usually the only companies that advertise this are startups with credit so bad they can't qualify for credit anyway. Or they are growing so slowly they don't need to be in debt. And others have debt and are lying about it.

Just about every company that experiences rapid expansion will experience cash-flow problems and need a line of credit to continue to grow. This is not just in Leveraged Sales...this is any industry. In fact, due to the exponential growth often experienced in this business, you could argue the case that there's even more reason to have a line of credit in Direct Selling than traditional companies.

In the early 1990s, I was building a program that put in more than 25,000 new, active distributors and customers in one month. Two months later, we put in 40,000 new, active people in a month. A short time later, 60,000 in one month.

The kinds of demands made on the parent company during exponential growth like this are mind-boggling. To expand distribution capabilities, to find and hire enough employees, and to simply locate and lease office space fast enough are monumental challenges.

Now figure what it takes to keep up with production in manufacturing products. Factories can't be built in two months. It can take a year to find the right site, draw up the plans, and pull the permits. Realistically, you have to start planning a factory three to five years before you need it. Depending on the breadth of the product line, machinery at the factory can cost millions of dollars.

So imagine having to add 50, 75, or even 100 employees in a month; paying for all the office space, desks, computers, training, and so on, they require; and investing millions of dollars more in a factory you won't need for two or three years. This is the challenge fast-growing Direct Selling companies face frequently. The company that can finance this kind of growth out of cash flow is one in a million. You could actually argue that to do so would leave the company's assets too tied up to handle any unexpected challenges that arise.

I hate debt. I was burdened with it for too many years. Nowadays, I try to encourage my people to pay cash for everything, including their cars, and even pay off their mortgage. Yet it still makes sense to keep a line of credit or some credit cards. Even if you don't use it, you never know when extenuating circumstances will arise and you will want to have some credit available. The same holds true for companies.

Imagine the dilemma placed on a company in the heat of exponential growth. Being completely debt-free might not be a good idea at all. I have seen this happen time and time again—companies grow so fast, they grow themselves out of business. Even as fast as they're growing, the money coming in is simply not sufficient to adequately finance the massive ramp-up in physical plant and operations that are necessary.

This does not mean the company shouldn't be properly capitalized. I believe the days when a successful Direct Selling company could be started in a basement or at a kitchen table are over. In my experience, it takes at least $15 million in start-up capital to launch a company today, because the Internet makes the whole world a neighborhood marketplace.

Even with this kind of start-up cash, it's possible that when the company hits "critical mass" and enters the exponential growth curve, it will need a line of credit or an infusion of more money to keep ahead of demand on production, personnel, manufacturing facilities, and offices.

A company with some debt and credit worthiness with a financial institution is a good sign. So, all told, finding a company that's debt-free is simply a nonissue. Let's spend some time unpacking the elements that truly are required for a company to become successful.

Management Depth

If the entire corporate staff consists of five people, the company will be hard-pressed to give any meaningful type of distributor support. A credible company should have a president and CEO (which may be the same person), a chief financial officer, a chief technology officer, a chief operations officer, an administrative manager, a distribution center manager, a customer service manager, and a marketing vice president or manager.

Some of these positions, even in a brand-new, start-up company, will require assistants and line employees. There may not be much for them to do when the company first opens. But the whole point in business is having the resources you need *before you need them.*

I especially look at what kind of marketing staff a company has. Do they have a marketing VP or national marketing manager? Do they have corporate trainers who travel around to the functions and conduct training? Is there a support staff to back up these people? What kind of customer service department do they have?

It's important to know if anyone on the corporate management staff has any successful experience in Leveraged Sales. Our profession is dramatically different from traditional business. If a management team doesn't understand the unique nature of our business, it will be quite difficult for them to guide the company.

When I consult with companies, this is the biggest issue they face. They have a management team with traditional corporate experience but who don't understand the distinctive culture of our business.

Support Structure

What kind of support structure is in place? Does the company have a robust website, individual replicated sites for distributors, and mobile apps? E-commerce is playing a dramatically larger role in our business and I believe many companies in our space haven't caught up to this.

Are there annual conventions, leadership training, and other events hosted by the company? Do they have regularly scheduled conference calls or webcasts? Are the materials professionally prepared, benefit-driven, and effective from a marketing standpoint?

This is where most companies fall down. And I do mean most companies, not just the start-up ones. They want to fund their growth through initial sales and aren't prepared to make the necessary investment before they sign up the first distributor.

The other big issue is they have no clue how to provide compelling marketing materials. The resources they offer are feature-driven, not benefit-driven.

Look at the materials of the company you're considering. Is the first thing you see the company logo? A picture of the founder? Pictures of the air handlers on the roof of the building? Are they filled with inane blather about how great they are, how old they are, where their officers went to school, and where they travel to get ingredients for the products? These things are all features and mean nothing to your candidates.

Make It About the Candidate...

Marketing materials, in order to be effective, must speak to the candidate. This means benefit-driven, not feature-driven.

If your brochure says, "We're an established 11-year-old company..." that's a feature. If it says, "Your future is secure, because we're an established 11-year-old company," now we're getting closer to benefits.

If your materials claim, "We have an automobile fund..."—that's a feature. If they say, "When you reach the Gold Director rank, you'll be awarded a new car..."—that's a benefit.

Here's a helpful way to know whether something is a feature instead of a benefit. If you can put the words "you get" at the front of the sentence, it's most likely a benefit. If you can't, it's probably not.

I once worked with a company that spent $250,000 (back when this was A LOT of money) on a new recruiting video. It was a 20-minute documentary of how many machines were in the manufacturing facility and how much each cost. "This machine, which puts the caps on each bottle, cost more than $500,000..." As you can imagine, many candidates slipped into comas and were never heard from again.

The effectiveness of the marketing materials you have to work with will dramatically impact your success. So evaluate them mindfully.

Evaluating Compensation Plans

There are some great compensation plans in practice today. And also some duds. And then, of course, there are also the pyramids, Ponzi schemes, and money games that attempt to portray themselves as legitimate opportunities. So how do you evaluate them?

Note: I must warn you that now we're going to get down and dirty. And a lot of what you're about to read may be more than you can process if you're a beginner in the business. But I feel it's important to include this information, so that the top leaders and corporate executives who have input into plan design have the benefit of this information. For most of you, you can skip over this section!

First, let's talk about the type of compensation plan it is. In my book *How to Build a Multi-Level Money Machine*, I broke down the different types of plans and looked at the benefits and drawbacks of each. I won't do that again for two reasons.

Number one: Comp plans have evolved greatly and the information is too complex for the average distributor or candidate to understand. Number two: Today there are so many plans that are hybrids and mashups of the four basic plans, analyzing them no longer makes sense.

Very few plans exist today that would qualify as one of the original four types. Around 15 years ago, we started to see more and more hybrid compensation plans. I believe this has been a very positive development and that these evolved plans offer the best results for all parties.

But before we leave this discussion of the four main types of plans…

I will specifically talk about one type. (Which will likely upset many of you and cost me a lot of book sales. But I feel it's important to state it.) That type is the binary plan.

Binary Compensation Plans

Binary plans were originally invented by scammers to take advantage of less-sophisticated distributors. The plans were so popular and created so much hype, legitimate companies started adopting binary plans or binary elements into their existing plans to compete. Binary plans can be great for creating big checks in the short term. And they are perfect to use if you want to create "sweetheart deals" for favored people.

The "bi" in binary is for the number two, as in everyone builds two sides of their organization. Most of the under-the-table (or sweetheart) deals being shopped around today give the recipient a "cooked leg." This means one side is automatically qualified every pay period, so that person has to build only one side. And often those people are allocated more slots where they can place people under them who also have a cooked leg.

Of course, no one discloses these backroom deals to the rest of the distributor force. They believe the examples of growth and income they see above them are the normal speed and financial rewards of the business. But that's a dirty, despicable lie.

If someone has a cooked leg, it's not just twice as easy to build to a rank. *It's more like 10 times easier to build to a rank,* because they can just keep placing everyone under everyone else, down one leg, which qualifies them and their people at higher ranks exponentially faster.

In the meantime, all the poor suckers down in the group are miserable, beating themselves up, because they can't understand why they aren't breaking ranks and cashing the big bonus checks like the people above them. What they don't know is—they never had a chance. Because they're not playing by the same set of rules.

Here are some other reasons con artists and other ethically challenged people adore binary plans:

- The top spots can all be assigned to privileged people.
- They create a lot of breakage, which funnels more money up to the company or top distributors with favored placement.
- Many companies cap the volume, requiring you to purchase more slots to access the volume in your group.

So because of these factors, and the fact that the vast majority of backroom deals use the binary plan, it has a very poor reputation among regulators. (And is illegal in some countries.)

Often customer acquisition is not emphasized in binary plans, because customer volume is usually not placed into either leg. Even when it is, binary payout mechanisms must be employed to reward the selling distributor. But the payout percentages of such mechanisms are insufficient to be worth the effort required. Binary plans are notorious for low effort-to-earnings ratios until the distributor reaches the higher levels of the plan. This causes binaries to have extremely high attrition.

I believe there are better ways to get the desired results in plans than though the binary mechanism.

Important Note: *This does NOT mean that all companies that use a binary plan or have a binary element in their hybrid plan are unethical or bad companies.* They are not.

I consult with several companies that have binary elements in their compensation plans and they are stellar examples of ethical operations. I would say there are at least seven or eight other companies that use complete binary pay plans or include a binary element in a hybrid plan, and they run exemplary organizations overall. What we really need to focus on is the end results.

The most important point to consider in evaluating companies and compensation plans is whether they have a clear focus on bringing in

customers. This is the true difference between Direct Selling compa-
nies and the shady deals operating in grey areas. And since we're being
honest here—I have seen all compensation plan types used to promote
sketchy behavior.

So while I'm not a big proponent of the binary ele-
ments, your main concern should not be the structure but
the *intention* of the compensation plan.

No matter what type of plan it is—whether binary, uni-
level, breakaway, matrix, or hybrid—if the focus on earning does
not come from selling to customers but rather by selling to distributors, the company and the plan will be or become illegal in
most countries.

Full Disclosure: I currently receive residual income from
the last company I built with, and it does have a binary compo-
nent in the plan. However, that doesn't stop me from recommending that we eliminate binaries—because I believe there are
more effective ways to compensate distributors. But at the end
of the day, what we should be most concerned with is paying distributors in a way that produces the best results.

Let's explore the key points that make a comp plan
work most effectively.

A Well-Designed Compensation Plan

A well-designed plan effectively meets the needs of three wildly
divergent entities: the customers, the distributors, and the
company.

First, the plan should provide incentives for customers to
order in bigger quantities or more frequently and, ideally, register for autoship. This is a new role for compensation plans. In
the past, plans were simply designed for the distributors and the
company. But as the profession matures and the regulations that
police it evolve, companies need to proactively take measures to
increase customer development.

Distributors will always seek to maximize their payout in a compensation plan. So it just makes sense to construct your plan in a way that fosters team members to build a large customer base.

Next, the plan must reward distributors for demonstrating the right behaviors: building a customer base, maintaining qualifications, and working in depth to support their team. This means *not* rewarding distributors to conduct behavior that isn't productive. (Like front-loading or having to sponsor so many people personally that they have no time to work with people on lower levels.)

Finally, the plan must ensure that the company is profitable. It is the "golden goose" for distributors. If the company doesn't maintain financial viability, it won't exist for either customers or distributors. Many distributors seem to forget this. So the comp plan has to be structured to allow for investments in research and development, marketing, and expansion—all while still providing a profit for shareholders.

In the overall view, here are the objectives of a well-designed compensation plan:

- Increase retail sales
- Simplify retail earning opportunity
- Allow new distributors to earn some start-up income quickly
- Increase company growth while maintaining profitability
- Reward correct long-term building behavior
- Provide some transitional income to bridge people during the time they are gaining experience and developing their skillsets
- Be competitive with other opportunities
- Provide seamless payments for sponsor lines in different countries

- Comply with new customer-centric regulatory requirements

- Simplify qualifying to empower more leaders to stay consistently qualified

- Create pathways for large retailers who don't recruit to achieve lifestyle awards

- Provide a platform for full-time professionals to create passive income

- Rebrand away from potentially objectionable terms like network marketing, MLM, millionaire, binary, and multilevel

- Design to be complex enough to promote the desired behavior, but simple enough for the concept to be explained in a 15-minute presentation

- Be a win/win/win proposition for customers, team members, and shareholders

So what are the best practices in terms of constructing a plan to achieve these objectives? Here are some key elements.

One of the biggest issues today—and the issue most overlooked in older comp plans—is the one I mentioned above. Successful plans need to possess effective strategies to distinguish and develop the customer base. This is done to both comply with legal issues and foster growth of the business. So, as an example, companies might build in increased customer requirements to access higher levels of the bonus payouts.

The other big change I recommend with new plans today is creating paths for distributors who are primarily retailers to take part in the lifestyle rewards of the plan.

For most companies, retailers have no path to qualify for perks such as the bonus car or travel programs. These rewards usually require extensive recruiting. However, forward-thinking companies should have alternate qualifications that can be attained by people who aren't building a team but create large sales through retailing.

What is the message your comp plan is sending to people if the fun perks like travel and bonus cars are available only to recruiters and not realistically accessible for retailers?

Essentials for a Solid Compensation Plan

As you can see in the previous list, I believe there should be three stages in a good plan:

1. Right-now money for beginners
2. Transitional income as people develop
3. Serious residual income for leaders

Here's the reality...

If you grabbed the first 100 people you find in line at an airport security checkpoint somewhere, you can safely bet the rent that at least 90 of them don't even have a savings account. Seventy-five of them would need to use a credit card if they had an unexpected expense of $400 come up. Savings are at an all-time low, and consumer debt is at an all-time high. So people need some upfront earnings.

When I started in the business, it was customary to earn anywhere from $5 to $25 for your first month in the business. (And you used this as great ammunition later when you were successful and shared your story. I "dined out" for three years on my story of earning only $3 my first month in the business.) Can you imagine trying to repeat that in today's environment?

People are more impatient than ever. The days when they will stick around while making $30 a month are a long way back in the rearview mirror. Most will have to put the start-up investment on their credit card, and they need to make it back quickly. So your plan has to offer some ways to do that, with a big part of that being retailing.

For the same reason, the "weeknight warriors"—the part-timers who are working 10 or 12 hours a week, still learning the business—need transitional income. This doesn't have to be huge. But there needs to be a pathway for them to get their monthly earnings to at least $300 or $400 quickly. That will allow them to fund their self-development, personal product consumption, and event attendance. This will keep them in the fold until they learn what they need to know to reach the high incomes and other perks.

The third criterion is a personal bias of mine. I always look for what elements of the plan can provide true passive income. I don't want to have to do things over and over each month. (That's why I don't work at the Pancake House any longer.) I want to do the job right, do it once, and continue to get paid every month. And there are a lot of others like me.

What you're doing in essence is creating "golden handcuffs" on your top leaders. Competition is fierce today, and many other companies now try to grow their business by stealing leaders from competitors. You want your top leaders locked in, so that jumping to another company just seems to be too much of an unknown and daunting variable.

Balancing Pay Across the Levels

Next, let's explore promoting the proper behavior and how the plan is balanced in relation to paying people at the various levels.

You need the plan to give people incentives for doing the right thing. That means the plan should not be skewed so all the money comes from bonuses provided by the volume produced by the initial enrollment orders. We want people working to produce volume all the time. And it's very important that the plan pays leaders for working down the organization in depth. This ensures that new distributors will get the support they need from experienced leaders.

The real nuance is providing the proper balance between the top and bottom of the pay plan. Some plans are top-heavy.

An example might be plans for companies that have only one or two products but have a high dollar level (like $10,000 or $15,000 a month) that someone must maintain to receive overrides on the leaders they develop. Due to the lower average volumes that they actually achieve, 99 percent of the distributors will never consistently qualify.

(In binary plans this may be evidenced by most of the commissions earned in the "running legs," so new people earn almost nothing. This is not true of all binary plans. Some have other factors to compensate.)

In top-heavy plans, most of the overrides roll up to a few poster boys and poster girls, or end up as breakage, and the money washes up to the company.

This can produce high six-figure monthly incomes for those poster kids at the top of the plan. But for each of these big earners, there are tens of thousands of distributors not making a monthly check big enough to pay their cell phone data plan. These big distributors can wave their mega checks around to hype growth initially, but ultimately most distributors will move on once they discover that they are not likely to earn any serious money. They will leave with a bad taste in their mouth and believe the business doesn't work.

On the other hand, bottom-heavy plans will not work long-term either…

These are plans where virtually anyone who joins can get high profits with minimal effort. They are designed in a way that over-rewards new people, with the hope that this will attract distributors from other companies to jump ship and come to the new company.

This excites people initially, but in the long term, the top leaders cannot make the incomes they deserve. They look at other plans and realize that with the exact same volume and same organization, they would make a lot more money in another company. This creates a leadership drain that ultimately prevents a company from succeeding.

You have only a finite amount of money to pay out. If you're overpaying the people on the bottom, it's coming out of the pockets of the people at the top. And vice versa.

To really balance a plan is a science. You want the beginning distributor to be able to start earning profit as quickly as possible, yet have the plan allow leaders to build up to and keep big-dollar incomes. Depth should be paid in proportion to width. (Meaning the more people you personally enroll should factor into how deep down your organization you are receiving overrides.)

If the plan is properly constructed, it contains all of the necessary elements to promote growth and pay people in proportion to the work they've actually done.

One more thought before we leave the subject of incomes…

Small Amounts Make a Difference

We have become jaded. Like, crazy-stupid jaded. If someone isn't pulling in at least $30,000 or $40,000 a month, an alarming number of people in our business look on that as a failure.

Yet we know that 80 or 90 percent of the bankruptcies today could be averted with a mere $300 or $400 a month in income.

Not to mention the fact that there are many places around the world where $300 or $400 a month is a *significant* income. In some of those places, that income actually makes them wealthy. And you can even argue that these modest bonus checks would also still make a huge difference to millions of people in the United States, the UK, and other developed nations.

In today's difficult economy, the Leveraged Sales profession is providing a lifeline of financial security to millions. At the time I'm writing this, $76 billion was paid to distributors in commissions the previous year.

Most people are not going to be earning $50,000 a month in the business. They're not willing to do the self-development and work that entails. *But as long as the plan rewards them relative to the work they actually do, then it's fair.*

Remember, even those $300 and $400 bonus checks are buying groceries, funding school or college costs, paying for medicine, supporting charities, making car payments, and keeping mortgages current. Let's not lose sight of that.

The Career Path

The critical element of comp plan design is having a clearly defined career path. All plans have ranks to achieve, and obviously there is a progression that people ascend. Sometimes those plans need to be thought out better.

The career path is the spine of your compensation plan because it determines the specific behavior the distributors will follow. When the career path is designed effectively, it guides the field through performing the behaviors that will cause them to become successful. When it isn't designed right, it actually inhibits or prevents true success.

The basic trajectory of a career path should accomplish two things:

1. Show distributors a simple and understandable "do this—get that" map to follow
2. Stimulate a continuous progression of rank advancement

Many compensation plans reward self-defeating behaviors by the nature of how the career path is designed. To create the proper behavior, the elements of the plan need to be coordinated together in a synergistic way. This is *very complex* science in my view, but let me give you a few examples so you know what we're talking about.

In many plans, a big part of the commission payouts comes from team commissions. But these team commissions aren't connected to the ranks or the career path. This creates negative behavior. Why would a distributor want to advance up the career path when no clear increase in earnings is given when they do? This will produce the wrong culture, which makes a headwind to sustain future growth.

Another example comes from the binary payout mechanisms. (Another reason why I don't like them.) They don't reward builders for developing leaders in their strong leg. And often the binary counts as a large part of the earnings potential, but a minimal or no part of the rank advancement and career path. In my experience, the more a plan depends on binary pay, the fewer leaders are developed. This has to be counteracted with other mechanisms to fill the gap, or a bad culture and mediocre results will develop.

When we are studying the effectiveness of a current plan or running simulations of a proposed one—a rule of thumb we follow is that at each succeeding rank, the number of people qualifying should be approximately half of those from the preceding rank.

So as an example, suppose your career path follows this rank progression:

Bronze, Silver, Gold, Emerald, Ruby, Diamond, Double Diamond, Triple Diamond

When you're looking at the actual payout, you'd want to see numbers in the neighborhood of these:

Bronze 4,000 distributors

Silver 2,000 distributors

Gold 1,000 distributors

Emerald 500 distributors

Ruby 250 distributors

Diamond 125 distributors

Double Diamond 60–65 distributors

Triple Diamond 30–35 distributors

A payout like that shows a balanced and attainable career path. Of course, this won't work out perfectly following this formula. But if we're not achieving close to this ratio, the career path is out of balance. (By the way, I'm showing only eight ranks here. An effective plan would usually have many more. This is just to show you the concept of how the progression should work, no matter how many levels there are.)

If we see that there are 250 Rubies and 224 Diamonds, it shows us that the qualifications required for Diamond are too low. On the other hand, if we see that there are 125 Diamonds, but only 18 Double Diamonds, then it shows us that the qualifications for Double Diamond are set too high.

You want to avoid dead spots between ranks, because it means the next step in the career path is so daunting that many people simply give up on achieving it and remain plateaued at a lower rank.

Lifestyle Rewards

When I consult with companies on designing comp plans, I always include lifestyle rewards like car bonuses and travel, because they have a very real effect on recruiting, retention, and distributor satisfaction.

The reason for the perks is they make recruiting so much easier for the average distributor. They don't always realize this, however…

If you ask most people if they would rather get $3,000 or a free trip to Hawaii, they'll opt for the cash 95 percent of the time. Then they'll pay bills with the money and it will be gone in

48 hours. But give them a trip to an exotic locale, and they will be snapping pictures, posting videos, and reliving that trip for years. It creates a lifetime experience that is anchored with your company. And it creates a buzz in their world…

When someone wins a cruise or other free trip, everyone they know hears about it. When you drive home in a new car and your neighbors find out you got it for free, they're panting to know how. So building these perks into the plan is one of the best investments a company can make.

Keeping the Trains Running on Time

The final factor to consider when choosing a company is how well they execute the basics. If a company does not ship product in a timely manner—and pay commissions on time every month—my advice is to move on. My experience is that if a company does not have the capital and resources to pay bills and stock product early on, it will only get worse as they get bigger.

Even the best companies experience problems in keeping up with inventory demand from time to time. While no one enjoys problems, these are the kind you like to have.

If a company is generally well run and ships out *the vast majority of its orders* on time, an occasional miscue should be overlooked. But when a company consistently does not ship product, pay its bills, or issue commissions in a timely manner, that is a sure sign of trouble.

Final Thoughts on Selecting a Company

You'll notice in every case, I used the singular version of company—not plural. I don't believe anyone can build two or more programs simultaneously. There are still too many MLM Zombies floating around. They're in so many crazy deals all the time, one or more of them is in the process of going bust. They use this as evidence that they should be in yet more deals—to diversify and protect their income. And they offer all sorts of convoluted logic to support this position.

> *"Company A has nutrition products—Company B has household cleaners, so they don't compete with each other. I need the Internet to build both of them, so Company C—a utility program—is the perfect complement. And Company D offers a free car program—which is perfect—because Company E sells car polish!"*

Even with two companies in which the products do not compete—the business opportunity does.

A Shell service station franchisee wouldn't open an Exxon station across the street. It would be foolish. Why compete with yourself? As Art Jonak says, "Doing one thing is hard. Doing two is way more than twice as hard."

Occasionally you will find someone who gets income from more than one program. But my experience is that if that income is substantial, it was produced working one program at a time. In other words, they built up one program and retired. Later, they joined another company and built a new network, never touching their people in the first organization. If you want to build a vacation home—it doesn't make sense to use the roof tiles from your existing house.

Working more than one program can look tempting. Discounts on all those products. Cashing so many bonus checks. All those different cars, trips, and awards you're going to win…

In actuality, those things don't happen. Each company's system contradicts the other. Because there are so many materials to buy, functions to attend, and training systems to learn, your distributors become confused and paralyzed into inactivity.

My advice: Take the time necessary to select the right program for you—then give it everything you've got, exclusively.

So what's your next step? Getting off to a lightning-fast start! Which is what we'll explore in the next chapter…

CHAPTER 4

The Secret to Lightning-Fast Growth

In some of the following chapters, you'll learn a lot of the micro—specific techniques and actions to grow your business, step by step. In this chapter I want to discuss the macro—the big-picture strategy and principles that will allow you to grow in the fastest manner possible.

Motivation and positive thinking will carry a new distributor only so far. Unless she has a believable, logical plan for attaining her dreams, fear and procrastination will take over. And the same will hold true for you too. So the purpose of this chapter is twofold: to get you off to a fast start and to teach you how to work with your new distributors so they get the most traction early on as well. Let's begin with...

THE MINDSET TO MAKE IT HAPPEN

I already told you that you make or break your new distributors in their first two weeks, and the first 48 hours are critical. This likely holds true for you as well...

If you get into action quickly and get some small successes, you're likely to stay around. If you spend your first few weeks "getting ready to get ready," you'll probably find yourself on a procrastination train and end up doing nothing until you eventually drop out.

If you spend that time scrolling through the company website, rewatching the recruiting video, and talking about what you're going to do but never doing anything—the two weeks go by and nothing has really happened. Your excitement fades and your dream gets further away.

Now, if during your first two weeks, you're learning the business, taking action steps, and actually getting some customers and builders into your group—momentum begins and your excitement level rises. (Remember what I said earlier about "study, do, and teach" simultaneously?)

> *Good work habits are created—which generate initial positive results—which motivate you to perform more good work habits.*

A REAL COMMITMENT

Please don't begin with the attitude that you will "try" the business. Come into it with the mindset that you will become a student of the profession and make a one-year commitment to becoming a professional.

Like any new occupation, Leveraged Sales requires learning new skills. The good news is you have the opportunity to earn as you learn. But the best advice I can give you is to reinvest everything you make in your first year or two right back into the business. And commit to one year of working your business only 10 to 15 hours a week before you make any evaluations. I believe that if you follow this duplicable system for that time, you will be so pleased with the results that you will continue the business for the rest of your life.

Here's another perspective on this. I was speaking with Andi Duli about this subject, and he had some strong feelings. He told me, "Personally, it took me almost that long to just see my first milestone. Never having run a business before, coming from poverty, I was infected with so many limiting beliefs and a poverty consciousness, I was almost nowhere after the first year. What I found helpful was seeing myself in the business 10 years from then. I saw the first year as building a foundation, but 10 years as building true wealth, becoming world class, and creating a life I would be proud of. Approaching the business with that long-term perspective helped me see that failure wasn't an option, and I weighed any challenges I faced at that time in lieu of where I could I be in 10 years."

Certainly Andi is glad he stayed around long enough to make it. And if you know my story, you know I lost money for five years. So make sure that your one-year evaluation is just that—an evaluation as to whether you are making progress and advancing towards your dream. It doesn't mean you're going to be rich and famous just yet. Mastery takes time.

BUILD THE FOUNDATION

(You have—hopefully—already taken the following actions. But run through the list and make sure you have.)

Activation Order Placed

This should be done at the same time you register as a distributor. You must use the products or services personally so you can get excited about them.

How much should you order? Somewhere between what you need—and where you're nervous. I say this only halfway in jest. Because "just what you need" is not enough.

You'll need some inventory for loaning to new distributors while they wait for their first order to arrive, extras for temporarily out-of-stock items, and samples to include with your follow-up packets. Make sure you have enough products on hand to build your business.

Some years back, I was working in a program that offered organic household cleaning products. One of the things I did with new distributors was to go through their house with them—removing all the "Brand X" products from their bathrooms and kitchens. We'd place all these in a shopping bag—replace them with the good stuff—and give away the old stuff to a worthy cause. This same concept will work for most programs.

It is critical that you use the products or services yourself and can testify to how good they really are. Also, you always want to buy from your own store. You never want to ever have a "Brand X" product in your home that competes with one your company provides. (Imagine the reaction of one of your team members or leaders if they see competing products in your home. And you can be sure they will check.)

Set Up Your Autoship

If your company has an autoship program you should be set up on this for a regular, ongoing order. This ensures you never run out of product and are always qualified for any commissions and advancements you earn. Autoship is the engine that keeps your business operating smoothly. It also allows the company to forecast demand to better ensure that products are in stock and available.

Don't think of this as an additional expense, because that is really not the case. Many of the products you use are actually "transfer buying" for items you would have paid retail for in stores. And depending on what your product line is, the long-term savings possibilities in other costs can be quite substantial.

Learn Your Back Office

Go to your company's website and log into your back office. Familiarize yourself with how to place orders, change autoship, and enroll new customers and distributors.

Connect with Your Sponsorship Line

Sign up for communications from your sponsorship team. This might be an email list, Facebook group, text, or WhatsApp group.

Review the Company Policies

Set aside a few hours of quiet time to read your entire distributor kit. Learn which sections to go to for specific information, and familiarize yourself with the Policies and Procedures and Code of Ethics for your company.

Apply for a Business Credit or Debit Card

Having a separate credit card shows you are serious about operating in a business-like way and also provides a great method to track your business expenses. Your accountant or tax advisor will thank you later.

Book Yourself for the Next Major Event

Most companies and organizations will put on two to four major events each year to help you grow your business. These events offer you information-dense training on the best ways to build your business. Some are only for the higher pin rank team members (like leadership conferences), while others, such as the company convention and other events, are for everyone—to help you reach those higher ranks.

These major events provide an opportunity for you to connect with the leaders in markets in which you may have some contacts and would love to have a group. So whether you want to build just in your home country or you want a business around the world, you simply must get to these.

Frankly, the people who attend these events have a serious head start on those who don't. They can cut months or even years off of your learning curve. You simply can't find any other substitute for being at these events live: talking to top producers and corporate executives personally, asking questions, networking during breaks, finding support buddies, and immersing your-self in success programming with the best and brightest people in your company. Not to mention, being able to post on social media, to show your team members who didn't attend how much they are missing.

These are the kinds of programs for which you would pay hundreds or even thousands of dollars, pounds, or euros if you could find something like it in a public seminar. (Which you can't.) If you didn't register for the next major event when you enrolled, correct that now.

Set Your Goals

You must decide what your ultimate goal is from your business. Are you just interested in getting your products free? Are you looking to make enough to cover your car payment? Or do you want to develop complete financial freedom? To reach your goals, you must first determine what they are—then set a timetable to reach them. This is your chance to make plans for your dreams.

Writing a short paragraph of your "why" will help zero in on what you want—to emotionally connect yourself with the rea-son you're doing the business in the first place. This will provide much-needed motivation when you face the challenges ahead.

This can help crystallize your goals a bit more and discover your "burn." It's this burning desire that will keep you focused and motivated during the early development stages of your career when challenges are greater and the income hasn't caught up to your effort. Keep that burn in front of you with a prosperity map or dream board. (Just use a large piece of poster board and place images of things you want to do, to have, to become.) This is the secret to staying self-motivated.

> *Goals are dreams with a deadline. So write them down*
> *and make sure they are specific and measurable.*

I believe that the average person, following a system, can achieve financial independence in this business during a two- to four-year time period. Think about what you want to do right away. Then think about what you'd like your two- to four-year plan to be.

Dream-build with your spouse and your sponsor. Reawaken those wants and desires you used to have but probably lost somewhere along the way. Sometimes we get so busy in the bustle of everyday living that we lose sight of our dreams.

Schedule Your Business-Building Time

The secret of rapid growth in our profession depends on how you spend the 10 to 15 hours a week you have allocated for your business. You want to include as many real business-building activities as you can and minimize "busywork." Mark off the time when you will hold meetings, conduct conference calls, and begin to contact candidates. If you plan your 10 to 15 hours a week ahead of time, you'll be much more productive.

Work closely with your sponsor to determine how to schedule your time for the first few weeks of your business. Find out the dates of all upcoming functions for the next 90 days so you can schedule them. Also, learn the dates of the annual conventions and conferences. As you saw earlier, these major events are critical to your success, and you want to make sure you can plan and arrange for travel and time off from work so you can attend.

I HATE TO WRITE IN ALL CAPS BECAUSE IT LOOKS LIKE I'M SCREAMING. BUT I NEED TO SCREAM ABOUT THIS!!!

Seriously. The difference in results between people who actually block off their 10-plus hours a week to really work their business—versus the people who don't—is colossal. This might seem like a little thing, but it is the foremost reality of your results. Scheduling and blocking off the actual hours you and your people will work the business will push up your productivity and results exponentially. Really.

Most people don't need bigger goals, but better daily habits.

Purchase Your Business-Building Tools

As with any business, you need certain supplies to operate efficiently and effectively. You will succeed much more rapidly and better duplicate that success with your team if you utilize the proven tools your sponsorship line recommends.

These tools are designed to provide your candidate with authoritative and credible information about the products and business opportunity in a professional manner. By using these third-party tools, you do not need to be an expert to start having success. Just point to the tool and let it do its job. This allows anyone to work the business effectively without special skills, talents, training, experience, or educational background. And using them makes a huge difference in your ability to duplicate. Also, please consider investing in my online leadership academy at www.gagevt.com.

Complete Your Candidate List

This is one of the most important steps. Do not skip it and do not do it halfway. Just start writing down the names of everyone you know.

Try not to prejudge: *Well, he makes a lot of money, so he probably won't be interested. She wouldn't look at this because she has so many college degrees,* and so on. A mistake like that can cost you tens of thousands of dollars down the road. So, don't prejudge, just get down the names.

Out of every 100, there will be three or four high-pin-rank executives, six or eight mid-range pins, and another 20 part-timers, along with many people who can become customers. (For the sake of simplicity and your understanding, I'll use the term "pin ranks" throughout this book. This means people who achieve rank levels in your compensation plan, whether they're called Diamond Directors, National Vice Presidents, or Master Coordinators. The name comes from the fact that distributors usually receive a pin upon achieving these ranks.) You don't know who is who... and it's often not who you think it is.

If someone is listed in your phone or email, if you send them a holiday card or you're friends with them on social media, they are someone you should be offering a chance to look at your opportunity. The same is true with those people whose services you use—your hair stylist, chiropractor, pool maintenance guy, and other people.

You need to avoid what happens 90 percent of the time...

You make a presentation and sponsor a new distributor. He's excited and dreaming of all the money, trips, cars, and other goodies he's going to get. He already has his first five distributors in mind. So you send him home and tell him to make a name list.

Since he already knows the five people he wants, he doesn't bother with the name list but calls all five people to invite them to the next meeting. Then he sits back waiting for the big bucks to roll in.

You probably think you have a potential star in the making. But realistically, this new person has a lot of things working against him.

First, he probably made invitations before he was ready. They weren't very compelling, and he'll likely have a very poor turnout to the meeting.

Second, he didn't use a tool for the invitation, so even if he did it well, it will be harder to duplicate. Make sure that neither you nor any of the people you enroll make that mistake. Get down at least a couple hundred names so you can let people sort themselves into the right categories. (Some will argue that everyone you need is already in your cell phone. I agree with that. But I still think that having a separate candidate list that you continually update produces the best results. Or if you have some kind of replicated website or mobile app, you may be able to import your phone contacts into a candidate list.)

A lot of new enrollees will tell you they don't know that many people. Not true.

The average wedding has 500 people, 250 on each side. Which makes sense, because the average funeral has 250 people sign the guest book. And this is not counting the dozens and dozens of casual acquaintances you know.

Here's the most important reason you need to have a robust, viable candidate list…

Posture. This doesn't mean standing up straight. It means you present yourself confidently and know the value of what you are offering. You aren't beseeching people for favors or begging. You're offering an opportunity that you have great faith in.

If you have a small list, this leads to tentative or fear-based approaches (weak posture). If you stop your list after the first five or six people you think are naturals for the business, you'll probably approach them with a poverty mindset. You're afraid to call even a few people, because if they don't get involved, you've already blown half your list.

If you have a large list, you have strong posture, approaching people with strength and confidence. If there are 200 people on your list, you won't get despondent and cranky if the first four aren't interested. You're still looking at 196 more, so it's a whole lot easier to stay positive and productive.

Hopefully, you've already taken each of these steps. Now let's look at the framework you will use to actually launch your business and create some serious momentum.

COMMIT TO DOING A MAJOR BLAST

I was able to increase the speed and scale of growing my business by a scale of 10 times by integrating a concept I dubbed the "Major Blast." It will give you a dramatic increase over the incremental way most people approach launching their business. The idea behind it is to go big right away instead of trying to tiptoe into the process.

Your primary objective at this stage is to get enough customers buying products and new builders recruiting that you initiate some serious momentum. This creates traction that makes it harder to quit than it is to stay. It gets you and your team into action—and profit—quickly.

The goal of your Major Blast is to get at least 80 to 100 candidates into your prospecting funnel at the beginning.

Please understand that this doesn't mean you have to sponsor 80 or 100 people or even make that many presentations. Just that you want to give them an offer to view a presentation to see if they are interested.

It's important that you get a large number of people looking at the business in the top of your recruiting funnel to ensure you get enough customers and business builders coming out the bottom of the funnel. The goal is to get into solid traction right away.

It may seem ironic, *but it is actually easier to build the business fast than it is to build it slowly.* When you start fast, you create excitement and momentum that spreads down your group. And by getting into a positive cash flow quickly, you set the tone for your team and create an exciting demonstration of success for candidates.

Like everything we're going to talk about in this book, the key here is using third-party tools to keep your efforts duplicable.

You do not need to use any hard sell, pressure, or hype. Just invite people, in a compelling way, to see a presentation.

Let the tools do the presenting. If your lips are moving, you should be directing someone to a tool. This can be a video, replicated website, catalog, or other form of marketing material. The objective is to edify the tool, then allow the tool to edify the opportunity for the candidate. This is what creates the best duplication for you.

The Major Blast is comprised of the following actions:

- Hosting a social get-together for creating your initial customer base
- Creating two or three business presentations to launch in your local market
- Executing an electronic campaign through email, SMS, and messaging apps
- Distributing mass-market recruiting materials in appropriate places
- Editing or creating your social media accounts to promote your business (more on this later in the social media chapter)
- Moving people from all of these funnels up the ladder to bigger presentations (both online and offline)

Now you have the macro, big-picture strategy. In the later chapters we explore the micro of the blast itself. Taken together with the rest of the items we looked at, the Major Blast really allows you to build your business dramatically quicker than most people ever achieve.

Maybe some of the basic and foundational things don't look sexy, but putting them into practice collectively creates a synergy for lightning-fast growth. And it all begins where we go next, how you construct a "bullet-proof," duplicable system...

CHAPTER 5

How to Construct a "Bullet-Proof" Duplicable System

It was about three in the afternoon when the call came in from one of my "siblings," another person cross-line who had the same sponsor as me. He was going through a belief crisis and needed someone to talk with about a fundamental issue of our profession. After stammering around about decoy issues, he finally asked the question that was troubling him.

"Does duplication really exist?"

He doubted this because he wasn't experiencing any duplication himself, even though he had been in the business for a few years. And then he confided that our mutual sponsor had recently told him, "Duplication is a mirage."

Some background: Our mutual sponsor was totally unduplicable. He had made his career "whale hunting," as he calls it. Pretty much his entire strategy is approaching successful distributors with other companies and convincing them to come over to his team. In fact, he had recruited the guy who was calling me in exactly that fashion. In his mind, duplication didn't really exist, because he had never been able to create it. Like a lot of people do, he took his own experience and projected it on the rest of the world.

Unfortunately, his experience is all too common in our space. Because too many people are introduced into the business in a way that produces very little duplication. I want to share with you how you and your team can build the business and create strong duplication at the same time. (I actually went on a two-year sabbatical and maintained my income during that time, so I can assure you duplication is real. Really, really real.)

To begin, we need to understand the dynamics that create and govern duplication. Some of them are principles, others are strategies, and others are…I don't even know. So I'm going to call them "truths." Once you completely understand these seven truths and how they impact your recruiting, you will experience a dramatic improvement in your duplication. Let's explore them.

TRUTH 1: IT DOESN'T MATTER WHAT WORKS. A LOT OF STUFF WORKS. WHAT REALLY MATTERS IS WHAT DUPLICATES.

At some point in your career, these words will resonate with every fiber of your being. And the sooner that moment comes about, the happier, healthier, and wealthier you will become.

When you understand the power of duplication, you'll make the breakthrough from being a grinder to a Leveraged Sales superstar. But superstar in the right sense—the duplicable way.

Our profession is filled with grinders. They may prospect on the benefits of residual income and leverage, but they don't actually get to live it. Because they don't understand the true meaning of those words above.

If you run a commercial at halftime of the World Cup, you'll sign up thousands of people. It would work. But how many people could duplicate you?

Many people think duplication is about them and their techniques and tactics. They think they can muscle their way to duplication, but that never happens. Duplication cannot be pushed; it has to be pulled.

> *You don't rise to the levels of your goals. You fall to the level of how duplicable your system is.*

TRUTH 2: IF YOU "DRIVE" LINES, THEY WON'T DUPLICATE. YOU HAVE TO BUILD THEM WITH PEOPLE AND PROCESS.

We can create hype and rah-rah. We can place people underneath other people in a way that causes them to rank advance sooner and without personal effort. But that kind of driving growth by hype can't be duplicated.

You have to be willing to perform the building block actions of bringing people in and training them how to get customers and recruit other builders by teaching them effective processes. These "safe space" processes protect them against unnecessary failures and dead ends.

Be willing to let go of the short-term quick fix and build for the long term. For every major decision you make, follow the philosophy of the Iroquois Indian tribe: Don't evaluate how it will affect your children or your children's children. Ask yourself how it will affect the seventh generation of children.

TRUTH 3: THE CLOSER YOU ADHERE TO "THE FORMULA," THE STRONGER YOUR DUPLICATION WILL BE.

So what's the formula? It is a three-part process that actually creates duplication.

> *Empower a large group of people to perform a few simple actions on an ongoing basis.*

Let's analyze the three parts. The first portion is having a large enough group. If it's only you and one or two other people, you don't have enough traction to get duplication going. You need to keep recruiting until you have sufficient critical mass to start the process.

The second part is performing a few simple actions. You have to dial this down to its most basic elements. Every increase in complexity creates a corresponding decrease in duplication. So you want *simple* actions. And they must also just be a *few* actions.

Then, of course, these actions must continue on an ongoing basis. You can't do a blast of energy for three weeks and then go missing in action for a month. Stay consistent and build a culture of consistency in your team. To create a successful business, people must consistently devote 10 to 15 hours a week to building the business, every week.

TRUTH 4: YOU CAN MAKE THE BEST DECISIONS ONLY IF YOU'RE WORKING FROM A VALID SAMPLE.

Pollsters make informed predictions for a large group of people by surveying a much, much smaller group. The key is to have a "valid sample"—meaning collecting enough responses to make sure the sample group accurately reflects the larger one. Our business is the same way.

If you live in Iowa, you may think the best time for a meeting is 5 p.m., because the people you know are farmers and they rise at 4 a.m. In Buenos Aires, you might think the best time for a meeting is 10 p.m., because most of your friends don't eat dinner until 8 or 9 p.m. Don't draw conclusions based only on your situation or worldview.

Just because the first two people you approached about your product line are allergic to soy doesn't mean that products with soy in them are not viable. And your four best buds from high school might think your products are too expensive. But if they're from the extremely low end of the socioeconomic group, that doesn't translate to the big picture.

Don't make any assumptions on anything until you have at least 1,000 people on your team. Even then, be mindful. And use the following question to set the guiding principle…

What is the most duplicable to the most people?

TRUTH 5: YOUR SYSTEM SHOULD BE BASED ON THE PREMISE THAT ALL TEAM MEMBERS PRACTICE THREE ACTIONS SIMULTANEOUSLY. THOSE ACTIONS ARE STUDY, DO, AND TEACH.

This is a first principle that I mentioned in the original edition of *How to Build a Multi-Level Money Machine*. And it's just as important today (maybe even more so). Move away from this at your own peril.

People naturally want to study everything for two months first. Then they think they'll take action. And then they figure that after they are rich and famous, they'll go back and train everyone how they did it. Of course, this works only in fantasy. Because even if it works to a degree (learn everything first)—then the people you bring in duplicate that process and growth takes too long. The time before people are earning anything of substance is so drawn out that your dropout rate increases dramatically.

You make or break your people in the first two weeks. And the first 48 hours are critical. So make absolutely sure that your new member orientation and system meet the standard of having people study, do, and teach simultaneously, right from the start.

TRUTH 6: MAKE ALL RECRUITING INTERACTIONS DEPENDENT ON A THIRD-PARTY TOOL.

Here's one of the most important things you will ever teach your team:

> *If you are in front of a candidate and your lips are moving, you need to be pointing to a third-party tool.*

Let's take this down to the most basic and simple example possible: Your customer candidate says, "I'm allergic to soy. Is there any soy in the protein shake?" Of course, you know the answer to that. But you don't answer. Instead you reach for a tool, in this case your catalog. You point to the ingredient list and say, "As you can see, there is no soy in the shake."

If they are thinking about doing the business, you've just modeled the perfect, duplicable behavior.

Because, subconsciously, they have just learned that to do the business doesn't require becoming a product expert who has memorized all of the ingredients. You just have to be savvy enough to know where to find the answers.

TRUTH 7: OPEN PEOPLE; DON'T CLOSE THEM.

One of the worst things you can do in our business is try to master closing and manipulative Neuro-Linguistic Programming (NLP) techniques. I believe that Leveraged Sales is governed by the ultimate universal law, which is…

> *The harder you close someone, the less they will duplicate.*

People you have to manipulate or arm twist to join will buy a kit, but they're the first ones to drop out. So stop closing people and start opening them.

Meaning simply present your case in the most honest but compelling way. Educate your candidate on all of the benefits they will receive from your product line and business opportunity, then let them make what they feel is the best decision for them.

If that means being a customer, great.

If that means joining the business, great.

If that means not joining in any capacity, great.

Thank them for their time and consideration and move on. If something in their life changes in the future, you may come back and revisit the offer with them. And if you treated them with class and respect the first time, they'll be all right with you coming back the second time.

DELINEATE THE SYSTEM

Back in the 1970s, franchising revolutionized the business world. The concept—which was quite controversial at the time—was that the parent company (franchiser) would provide a complete business system, including site selection, operating procedures, purchasing requirements, and employee training. They offered this expertise and a complete business model for an upfront investment and ongoing royalties on sales.

The person who licensed the business (franchisee) gave up a percentage of their profits but dramatically increased their chance of business success. These were dubbed "turnkey" businesses, because you could simply turn the key to unlock the door and be open for business. There were step-by-step procedures to follow for each facet of the business, from the simplest detail (what brand of straws to use) to the most complex (how to lay out the kitchen equipment for maximum productivity).

McDonald's, of course, was then, and still is, the consummate example of that. Go to any of their stores at 7 o'clock in the evening and you're likely to find it being run by a 19- or 20-year-old who just recently graduated from teenage acne. It's possible this kid has a mother who won't let him borrow her Volvo because she doesn't trust him with it. Yet this same kid is successfully running an operation that probably does in excess of $10 million a year in sales. What's the secret?

The Secret is the System

One of the most complete, specific, and tested systems ever developed. A system that can turn any 15-year-old into an effective, efficient, productive employee. One to three items go in this size bag; four to six items go in the next larger size. Here are the napkins you use; here's where you get them from. This is the day of the week you order supplies; this is when they'll be delivered.

You see the same thing in the military. Nineteen-year-old kids are flying a fighter jet that cost more than the gross national product of developing countries. But there's a preflight checklist, an in-flight checklist, a postflight checklist, probably a checklist just for the checklists.

Having this kind of system to follow created a quantum leap in the success ratios of start-up businesses. Today, as then, franchises have a dramatically higher level of success than independent businesses. And the same thing is true in Leveraged Sales. The organizations with the best systems produce the best results for their members.

A duplicable system is the roadmap for how success is created in your company. It should completely delineate and spell out the entire process that a distributor will follow: where to find candidates, how to approach them, how to sponsor them, and how to train them to reach the higher pin ranks. Each stage in this process should be clearly defined and taught to the distributor at the appropriate time.

If you're fortunate, a system will already be provided for you. Some of you reading this will be involved in the process of creating the system for your team. If you are a top leader in charge of setting up the duplicable system, these are the four important aspects to analyze and consider:

1. **What is the process?**
   How many steps are there and what are those steps? How does the process diverge in the customer candidate and business candidate paths?

2. **What are the tools?**

    Every stage in the process should have a corresponding tool (video, audio, brochure, catalog, product samples, etc.) linked to it.

3. **Have you set up a ladder of escalation?**

    Think of this as your prospecting pipeline. Meaning the process (presentations and corresponding marketing tools) that you pull candidates through as they evaluate your business.

    I use the term "ladder of escalation" because I believe you want the process to escalate at each step—that is, each step is always a bigger deal for the candidate than the preceding one. So this needs to be spelled out for each step—which action to take and the marketing materials that accompany each action.

    So, as an example, this progression might be:

    One-on-one presentation or watching a video

    Home meeting or ZOOM presentation

    Hotel meeting

    Worldwide live-streaming presentation

4. **How do I make this scale?**

    That's the ultimate objective of a system: To facilitate growth in a scalable way. For all of you guys who adore corny acronyms, think of SYSTEM as standing for *Save Yourself Stress, Time, Effort, and Money!*

So always be looking for ways you can automate activities. Do you really need to meet with each new team member one-on-one for two hours to begin, or could they watch an orientation video or follow along in a workbook? Do you have to meet with five different candidates at five different coffee shops, or could they all watch an online presentation at once?

Components of a Duplicable System

Here are what I consider to be the most important components of a duplicable system:

- **Standardized Presentation Outline.** Every presentation, whether online or offline, large or small, should still follow the same basic flow.

- **Physical Presentation Tool.** This might be a flash drive, flip chart, or another other tool that someone can hold in their hands and use to present to a candidate in a coffee shop, home, or conference room.

- **Online Presentation Tool.** There needs to be an option for the digital world. This could be a permanent video hosted on a website or scheduled live-streaming presentations.

- **Mass-market Prospecting Tool.** Everyone today is enamored with saving money by doing everything digitally. But ideally you should have some kind of a lead generation tool that a team member can leave behind—in places like the table in the dentist's office or the seatback pocket on an airplane.

- **Quantified Ladder of Escalation.** Already mentioned earlier. You need this process in place, so every time a candidate moves up a step, there is more validation and psychological proof that this is a great decision to make.

- **Standardized New Member Orientation.** It's vital that every new team member goes through a customary orientation to learn the basic need-to-know stuff like how to order, use the back office, enroll people, contact customer service, and other essential actions like that. And, of course, you want to get new members into action right away and build the culture of study, do, and teach simultaneously.

Some Final Thoughts

You might be competing against someone who has more contacts, better influence, and superior skills than you do. However, if they rely on those advantages but don't follow a duplicable system—and you *do* follow a duplicable system—you can eventually out-earn them.

I've given you seven truths above about duplication and creating a system to foster that. Now let me reveal to you the ultimate truth about this topic.

> *You haven't created the perfect duplicable system when there is nothing else to add to it. You will have created the perfect duplicable system when there is nothing left to chisel out of it.*

Now, if you are one of the leaders or company executives responsible for creating the system for your team, what you've just read is deep. On a lot of different levels. So please come back to this chapter frequently. Ponder the questions I raised to ensure you are really breaking down the steps, keeping them as simple and duplicable as possible. The corresponding results will be magnified exponentially for you, for many, many years to come.

Next up, you'll discover how to build a gargantuan customer volume…

CHAPTER 6

Building Gargantuan Customer Volume

If you're a real estate agent, you wake up every morning unemployed. Kind of sucks, doesn't it? It sure would be nice to wake up and have some income already earned for yourself, wouldn't it?

Yet a surprising number of people in Leveraged Sales wake up in a similar scenario. They rise every day having to chase another rabbit to eat. This is usually caused by one of three bad scenarios:

1. They may have built their business solely by whale hunting and their whale jumped into another ocean.

2. They forgot that leverage works only when there is something to leverage. They focused so much effort on signing people who want to recruit others that they created a strong culture around that, and no one was developing a customer base.

3. They started with customers but ignored them. They spent so much energy looking for recruiters that their customers felt neglected and drifted away.

Let's revisit the fundamental truth I mentioned at the start of the book. Everything in the pay plan and the profitability of your business is dependent on the volume produced by your products or services reaching the end consumer. Everything.

And not just that these products reach the end consumer. But that the end consumer pays for them, is satisfied with them, and reorders them again and again.

As you know, a great deal of those sales will be to distributors who buy from their own store and use the products themselves. Great. But that's not enough. For both legal and financial reasons, you need to develop a vibrant base of customers who aren't building the business.

Lots of people will benefit from your products or services but not be interested in building a business at this time. These people are the basis for your consumer group.

To begin, set a goal to develop a base of at least 10 retail customers. (And this metric should grow as your time in the business increases. As it will for your team. Which ultimately creates even more leverage.) *You want to be continuously growing your customer base and building it up to create a gargantuan volume.*

Here is another really intriguing aspect to consider: Recruiting ebbs and flows. Certain times of the year (like just after New Year's) are usually busy times for recruiting business builders. Other times, you're going to experience downturns. If you live in the West, the holiday season during the last two or three weeks of December is a much tougher time to recruit. Other factors, such as the local economy, civil unrest, or a multitude of unforeseeable events, could cause your enrollment numbers to plateau or dip.

So enrollments go through growth and diminishment cycles. They just do. But guess what? The sales volume of customers on an auto-refill program never wavers. So when you build up a strong customer base, those sales cover you and buy you time during recruiting dips until things pick up again.

In Chapter 4, I introduced the concept of the Major Blast. If you remember, one of the elements of that is:

A social get-together for developing your initial customer base.

Let's look at how that works. This was something one of my leaders in Italy tested and it worked out so well, we ended up adopting it team-wide. The concept is simple: You invite the 10 people who love you the most to your home. And you let them know you're announcing the "grand opening" of your new business. Explain what the product line is (using tools, of course), and let them know that you want them as a customer.

This is more simplistic than it looks—and also more profound...

What's the first thing anyone who gets an insurance license does? He alerts all of his friends and family that he is now selling insurance and asks that if they plan to buy a policy to call him. (How many times have you seen a post like this in your Facebook feed in the last couple years?)

What's the first thing someone does when they become a massage therapist? If your sister-in-law, neighbor, or bowling teammate opens a new restaurant, what's the first thing she does?

Exactly.

These people ask others they know to be one of their first customers. So you are simply repeating this time-tested, highly successful strategy to open your own new business. And if you make these announcements the right way, then you will have some fun and profitable get-togethers. Much more social than formal.

If you have weight loss products, by all means mix up some different recipes of smoothies and snacks and let people try them. If you have makeup or cosmetics, do some beauty makeovers or offer a fun, how-to class. Use videos and other tools, such as catalogs or brochures. Have your sponsor there or streaming in on the Internet. This should definitely be more house party than business presentation. No high-pressure pitches or closing techniques.

Remember, you're simply duplicating the same process someone uses when they get their insurance license or open a restaurant: Telling the people they know about their new business and how they would love to have their family and friends as customers.

Now if your first reaction is that you don't want to make money off your friends, you need to completely rethink that. According to my extensive research—your enemies probably don't do business with you. Next to consider is whether you really believe in your products. Because if you wouldn't want the people who love you the most to purchase them, you're probably in the wrong company.

Or else you simply have low self-esteem and feel squeamish about charging anyone for anything. If that's the case, you're going to need to deal with those worthiness issues or you'll never be successful.

In rare cases, you might sponsor someone who tells you they don't want to approach their friends and family. If that happens, I suggest you find someone else to work with, because you will be wasting both their time and yours.

VOLUME-BUILDING TIPS

Here are some valuable tips that can strengthen volume for you and your team.

Have a Killer "Turn" Question

You're inevitably going to approach lots of people about joining your business. A fair number of them will enjoy their current job or business, think having a second business demeans them, or simply not be ambitious enough to do more with their life. So if they signal that they're not interested early on, have a question or statement to "turn" the conversation toward getting them as a customer.

> **Example:** "I asked because I have a business helping people live better lives through breakthrough nutrition. Is that something you'd be interested in?"

> **Or another example:** "I brought this up because I have a business helping people save about 20 percent on their utility bills. Would you be interested in saving on your electric, phone, and Internet bills?"

Deliver Their First Order to Them Personally

Obviously, this isn't possible with every company, depending on the particular product or service. But if it does work for yours, this can be a powerful way to cement a strong relationship with your customers. Sometimes people receive a first order and, if it has multiple items in it, they'll let it sit there until they "have time to go through it all."

So the whole box sits unopened and unexplored for two weeks until they ask you whether they can get a refund. If you come over and open up the box, take everything out of the wrapping, and demonstrate exactly how the product is used/prepared/enjoyed, you'll have a much higher stick rate.

Have Price and Value Comparisons

Does your company sell concentrated formulas? You'd better have some data on that. Be able to show customers your gallon of window cleaner that sells for $15 will actually produce the equivalent of 10 bottles of regular window cleaner sold in the supermarket. Otherwise, don't be surprised if your customers compare your $15 product to a $4 one and stop buying from you.

Does your protein powder cost more than the stuff at the health food store? You better be able to show it's more bioavailable or has a higher potency.

Keep a Tickler File for Follow-Up

Check in with your customers in the first few days to see if they have any questions and are satisfied with their purchase. Know when their product will run out and reach out to them for a reorder before that.

Stock Sufficient Basic Inventory

I realize pretty much every company stocks and ships the products direct today. But that shouldn't preclude you from stocking some inventory yourself. When you have a new team member enroll, do you really want them waiting four or five days before they receive their first order? How much quicker will they build if you loan them some product immediately, so they can experience it and start developing their own product story or testimonial?

You need enough inventory to offer adequate samples to people after presentations. When you're working out at the gym and someone asks you what's in your shaker bottle, you want to have some of that in your car trunk, gym bag, or locker to offer them right there. When your friend from out of town asks how you keep your skin so radiantly beautiful, you want to have a jar of moisturizing cream she can take home with her.

See If There's a "Killer" Product Demonstration for Your Presentations

Here are some of the best examples of those I have seen or employed myself over the years...

- For a cleaning products company, put black shoe polish on a piece of white carpeting. Spray on the cleaner and wipe off the polish.

- For a nutrition company, put a famous name-brand vitamin in a clear glass of water. Put your water-soluble vitamin in another clear glass. Leave them on the lectern the length of the entire presentation. At the end of the night, bring people's attention back to the glasses to demonstrate that your vitamin is completely dissolved, and the still-solid Brand X vitamin most likely is just passing through people's digestive track without providing any nutritional value.

- For a weight loss company: If you lost 20 pounds with your products, ask the butcher at your supermarket for

20 pounds of the fat they trim from meats. Bring it in a plastic bag to your presentations and hold it up to your stomach (or your butt) for an eye-popping demonstration of the results they can achieve with your products.

- For a utilities company: Suppose your services save the average consumer $25 a month. What if you made a chart showing what would happen if that $25 was put in a savings account with compound interest over 10, 20, and 30 years?

- What about creating a Facebook, WhatsApp, or other social media group with regular updates on tips, testimonials, and helpful info about your products and what they do for people? (Much more about this in Chapter 9.)

Smother Your Customers with the Personalized Attention They Won't Get Anywhere Else

If you're in Young Living, your competition isn't dōTERRA. If you're in Nu Skin, your competition isn't Rodan + Fields, Mary Kay, or Arbonne. If you're in Herbalife, your competition isn't Isagenix, Nature's Sunshine, or Amway. Your biggest competitor is probably the cell phone in your pocket.

In an online interview, John Milton Fogg asked what I thought the biggest challenge the Direct Selling business was facing.

Instead of answering him, I turned to my Amazon Echo device and said, "Alexa, I want to buy a vitamin."

She responded, "Here's what I found. Based on your order history…"

I interrupted her and said, "Alexa, buy that vitamin."

The whole transaction took about 11 seconds. John stared at me, totally gobsmacked.

"That's your biggest challenge," I told him.

And now I'm telling you. Amazon, Shopify, eBay, and all those other online marketplaces are the biggest threat to our profession. You have to show your customers that you are their number one coach, guide, and mentor—and that no one in the world will take better care of them than you do.

THE LEVERAGE FACTOR

As you can see, you have lots of avenues for building your customer base and increasing your volume. This is good business, because you earn retail profits, develop residual income, and build group volume that will qualify you for faster rank advancement and higher rewards. What's really sexy is how this plays out as your group builds depth. This is when the magic of leverage will be demonstrated exponentially.

Let's suppose you have a group of 27 people who are all loyal distributors who love and use the products themselves. The average monthly consumption of this group is $75 per distributorship. You've got a group volume of just over $2,000 that everybody's commissions and overrides will be drawn from.

Now let's factor in everyone that has at least 10 retail customers...

Suppose the average customer spends $45 a month. The math comes down to $(27 \times 75) + (27 \times 10 \times 45)$. Now you've got a group volume of more than $14,000 that everybody's commissions and overrides will be drawn from. *That's a huge jump in potential earnings for that exact same group of 27 distributors.*

Wanna get really sexy? Play it out with a team of 500 people...

If you have 500 team members each consuming $75, you've got a volume base of $37,500 that all the commissions and overrides are based on. Again let's factor in a customer base of 10 each. Look at the math now: $(500 \times 75) + (500 \times 10 \times 45)$. Now you're looking at a volume of more than $250,000 that the commissions are drawn from. *From the same number of distributors.*

When you play it out in large teams of 10,000, 20,000, or larger, the numbers are mind-boggling. Which is why we have leaders in our space earning incomes most people are afraid to even dream of.

> *When you build a strong customer culture, you are leveraging your leverage.*

One more consideration: What I've shared here are some strong strategies to get your team attracting a lot of customers. There is a flip side to this. You need to make sure those who want to build a team don't so over-index on acquiring customers that they lose sight of the team-building side of things.

Many people come into our space because they love the products and try to build by being a product expert. *Experts don't duplicate.* If you're not mindful, people will see themselves as health coaches, beauty gurus, and so on—and not as business builders. Keep them focused on letting the third-party tools be the expert, so they are able to duplicate.

In the next chapter, we'll dive deeper into how you combine your new product leverage with a strategy to prospect the best talent for growing your team...

CHAPTER 7

How to Prospect Brilliant Talent

A s I hurried out of my house, I stopped to pull out my cell phone, and punched in my mother's number. Unfortunately, I got her voicemail. So I left the following message:

> "Hello, Mrs. Gage. I just want you to know that your son is on his way to have lunch with the president of the United States. Love you, bye."

My mom raised three kids, by herself, knocking on doors, selling Avon products. And this was back in the day. Not like today, where someone takes a catalog into their office and asks their coworkers if they want to order anything, or they post catchy memes on Instagram. My mom went house by house, apartment by apartment, literally knocking on doors to support her three kids.

I wish I could tell you that I appreciated my mother's effort at the time and understood the sacrifices she made to take care of us. But that would be a lie. Finding my purpose and how I wanted to live my life was a tortuous process, for both her and me. I was a teenage alcoholic and drug addict, which led to a lot of poor choices. Things came to a head when I celebrated my 16th birthday in jail, awaiting trial for armed robbery.

I was fortunate to have people who cared for me and reached out to help, allowing me to alter the trajectory of my life. So in 2012, when I left her that message, it was for one simple reason. *I wanted her to be proud of who she was and what she had done for me.*

Any time I face a difficult decision these days, I stop to take a breath and ask myself: Will what I am doing make my mother proud?

So why am I telling you all this?

Because that is the best advice I can give you about building a business. Build one you'll be proud of. Build one the people who raised you will be proud of.

PRACTICING GOOD ETHICS

I mentioned earlier how we need to get away from all the hype, manipulation, and questionable practices. Please understand that while some of those business tactics are effective short-term, they won't take you to where you ultimately want to go. I bet a lot of people would be surprised to learn that the moral and ethical approach is actually the most effective one from the standpoint of marketing and building a strong business. So before we get into the micro of how to prospect, let's look at the macro of the ethics involved.

Yes, we're all competing with each other. You're competing against many other companies that want the same candidates you have. You're even competing with other team members in your own company. You could even find yourself in a situation where you, your sponsor, and one of your personal enrollees are all competing for the same candidate.

But before you fall into a siege mentality, a little perspective helps. At this moment, there are 7.7 billion people on this planet. (And according to the estimates of the United Nations, there will be a net gain of 14 more during the time it takes you to read this chapter.) The overwhelming majority of them are *not* in the business. You don't need all of these people in your team to own a profitable business. You don't need half of them, a third of them, a fourth or them, or even one half of one percent. (Personally, I'd be happy if I had just two million of them on my team.)

So fighting over the pie—chasing the people who are already in the business—is pretty foolish. Wouldn't it be really clever if we all focused on baking a bigger pie?

Let's all agree to compete with integrity with other companies in a spirit that serves the profession as a whole. We can do this with fair market differentiation, not by disparaging other companies. Instead of talking about what you think is bad about everyone else, speak about what you think is great about your company.

When talking with a candidate, answer questions directly and without deception. (Using a third-party tool, if you're smart.) If you don't know an answer, don't make one up. Promise to find out the answer and get back to them with it.

Honor the governing laws in your jurisdiction regarding product and income claims. There's no need to exaggerate income examples. As my friend Dana Collins always says, "The truth is good enough."

Don't resort to job-shaming, education-shaming, or manipulation. Don't distort or attack. It really isn't necessary to close, hype, or hard-sell people. Genuine long-term success is all about solving problems and adding value. If you change your focus from what you want to sell, and instead focus on how you can solve problems or add value for your candidates—you'll achieve much greater success.

And one more thing…

Let's get all that silliness about fear of rejection out of the way, once and for all. Most people aren't thinking about you and your business. Not. Even. A. Fleeting. Thought. Even the people who know you and love you. They are thinking about the issues they're facing in their own life. The bills they need to pay… What's coming out this week on Netflix… Their next dentist appointment…

So when you call them and invite them to watch a video, come to a meeting, view a webcast, and so on—they'll consider what you ask. Say yes or no. Hang up and then three seconds later reach for the TV remote or be watching a video of some cat riding a Roomba vacuum cleaner.

So why don't you just get on with it and extend your invitation?

Would you like to know who are *the best, most-qualified candidates* for your business? That answer is easy. *It's the ones who enroll and get to work.* So how do you discover the people who enroll and get to work? That's even easier. *They are the people left after the others say no.*

Now let's talk about how you develop the mindset of an elite-level recruiter...

DEVELOP THE MINDSET OF AN ELITE-LEVEL RECRUITER

You might need to reprogram your mindset. Stop pondering questions like:

- Who can I sell this stuff to?
- How can I manipulate people into doing this?
- Who can I get to sell this stuff?

Start reflecting on questions like:

- Who really needs these products?
- Who can I help with this business?
- How can these products or this business opportunity add value to the people in my world?

If you're going to be successful in this business, you better own it and have some swag. You better know the true value of what you have to offer. Then I want you to pose the real question. The question you should really be asking each and every day of your business is:

How can I best recruit the kind of brilliant talent I'm looking for on my team?

Once you have that mindset, you're ready to do something extraordinary. *Yoda voice:* Only then, to proceed with your training, are you ready...

For you to become an expert at prospecting, you're going to need to become proficient at a few basic skillsets. The first of these is the skill of meeting new people.

Why is this important?

Because you don't already know everyone who is going to help you create success in the business. In fact, no one who joins our business already knows all the people they need.

Everyone comes into the business with their current list, the people they know. And how you do with that list depends on how your relationships with those people have been up to then.

Some people could start off with a list of 25 people and enroll 18 of them. Others start with a list of 200 and not even get in 8. Why?

It's often not their invitation skills. *It's how they interacted with that list before they ever joined the business. That's the good news and the bad news.*

When I started in Direct Selling and began working my list, my results were terrible. Why? Because I wasn't very well liked. My interactions with many people I knew weren't pleasant for them, and the last thing they wanted was to have to spend more time with me. I had no credibility, likeability, or trust built up in the "bank account" of most of these people.

When I came back into the business after a break, my list worked very well for me. Why? Because I had grown a great deal as a person. At that point, my relationships with people were built on mutual respect and adding value. Yet even though I had good relationships the second time around, I still needed to meet new people.

And so do you.

I've earned millions of dollars in commissions. And way more than half of that is from volume produced by people I didn't know when I began. And if you poll 10 elite leaders, 9 or maybe even all 10 will tell you the same thing.

The quality of your relationships with people in the past will intensely impact how well your invitations work with them when you begin. For some of you, like me, you'll need the personal growth that comes from the business to do well from your first list. You may actually do better with new people you meet, because you can start fresh today with those people.

This area is where we find the delta between the amateurs versus the professionals, the successful people versus those who quit without ever making it. The amateur makes excuses around the type or number of people they know.

Meeting New People

The professional who creates success understands that meeting people is a skill—one that can be learned.

Some of you reading this are a people person and a natural extrovert. You can skip the next few paragraphs. Others are introverts and shy about meeting new people. As someone who entered the business as an introvert with social anxiety (and still sometimes deals with those anxiety issues today), I would like you to know there are some great ways to meet new people in a very nonthreatening way.

The most important dynamic I find is a shared experience or commonality. If you're walking down the street wearing a

New York Yankees jersey and someone else is walking toward you, also in a Yankees jersey, they're probably going to greet you pleasantly.

If you're walking your mutt at 6 a.m. and someone else is out with their pooch, you'll probably strike up a conversation effortlessly.

And—you can bet the keys to everything you own—that if you're pregnant or pushing a baby in a stroller and encounter someone in the same situation, within three seconds you'll be chatting with them like you've known each other for 30 years.

This is because you have a shared experience, which creates an immediate bond. The same thing happens when you're standing in line to see the latest Marvel superhero flick, or you get out of your blue Camry as someone else pulls up next to you in a blue Camry.

One day I had the bright idea to join a softball league. So I responded to an ad and got picked up by a team. On my way driving to the field the first time, I started having an anxiety attack, because it dawned on me that I wouldn't know a soul there. But my desire to start playing softball was greater than my fear of meeting strangers at the moment, so I kept going. I've since earned literally millions of dollars in commissions from business lines I developed from people I met in that softball league.

> *Think about places and activities that you would enjoy so much—your joyous anticipation will be greater than your fear.*

Some great places to meet excellent candidates are classes at spiritual centers and continuing education, language clubs, sporting leagues, public seminars, and online groups and forums.

My "secret weapon" location to meet great candidates is at hand car washes. The people using that service have nice cars, which means they're probably ambitious, successful people. They are willing to pay more for a hand wash so their car doesn't get all scratched up. That means they're intelligent and willing to invest in what's important to them. They usually are "car people," and as they're standing around, waiting for their car to be finished, they're chatting with the other people about their cars.

Some important points to remember:

- In the beginning, you will get paid for who you were before you joined the business.
- The great candidates aren't in your home. The people who live there are already in, or they aren't good candidates.
- It's called "relationship marketing." But as Wes Linden likes to say, "The relationship comes before the marketing."
- Don't wait to get through your first list. Meeting people should be a continuous process.
- You can always change the equation by going out and meeting some new people today.

The three key takeaways for you are:

1. Meeting people is a skill.
2. It's a skill you can develop.
3. Success follows when you meet people and let the relationships develop naturally.

Don't try to make a presentation while you're waiting in line for the new *Mission Impossible* flick or hawk a distributor kit in yoga class. Meet people and start relationships. Then add them to your candidate list. Which leads us to the second skillset you need to develop—working a candidate list.

Working a Candidate List

We're not talking about *making* a candidate list; I assume you already did that. I'm talking about *working* one. Candidate lists should be organic—a living, breathing entity. It isn't something you write once, then put away in a drawer. (That's what amateurs do.) A professional updates their list every week.

That's because every week you probably meet somewhere between 7 and 15 people. The new clerk at your dry cleaners, someone hired at work, the neighbor down the street, and people at social events like a dinner party or baby shower. In the course of your Internet surfing, you're probably meeting even more. Most people just go through their regular routine and don't give any of this a thought because it doesn't happen at the exact time they're working their business.

But if you're approaching your business in a professional way, you're always mindful of everyone you meet and adding them to your candidate list. As people join your business, you take them off your list. And if someone goes through a presentation and declines the opportunity, you either remove them altogether or shift them to another list to check back with in the future, if something should change in their life. To be a master recruiter, you need to be able to play your candidate list the way a virtuoso plays the violin.

Extending an Invitation

The third basic skillset that factors strongly in your recruiting results is your invitation skills. *If we wanted to assign value to skillsets, your skill at inviting would easily be the most lucrative one.* The better you are at this, the more successful you will become. Because inviting is the nexus of everything we do. You invite people to one-on-ones, home get-togethers, hotel meetings, and online presentations. So let's go into depth on how to make compelling invitations. (Then in the following chapter, we'll discuss how to handle the actual presentations you're inviting people to.)

You know that, as part of your Major Blast, you're going to be inviting people to two or three in-home launch meetings. Then you want to do an electronic campaign through email, text, and messaging apps. So let's start with how you can get the most people to attend your launch presentations.

Inviting is all about your posture and connection. Weak posture equals low acceptance. Obnoxious posture produces a lower response than a weak one. You need a strong but friendly posture. Your candidate has to experience a direct correlation between what matters to them right now and what you are inviting them to do.

The three traits for successful inviting are passion, intensity, and urgency. These traits are required because of a simple but profound truth: Candidates don't know what they don't know. (And frequently, they don't know what's in their own best interest.) So sometimes you're going to have to exercise a little tough love with them. For an invitation to be compelling, there has to be an element of intrigue. So you can't reveal everything, no matter how persistent the candidate is.

When you have a candidate who absolutely won't back down and demands that you make the entire presentation in your invitation call, shut it down and move on to someone else.

10 Keys to Successful Inviting

1. Always make your invitations over the phone. The reason for this is simple. If you do them in person, that gives people the opportunity to start interrogating you. They often try to badger you into explaining the whole program right there. It's easier to extricate yourself from a phone call.

Here's the other powerful reason for doing phone invitations. Hardly anyone makes phone calls anymore; they've moved to texting or using messenger apps. As a result, your candidates don't get many calls. So when they do get an actual, you know, twentieth-century-style phone call, they assume it's something important.

2. Get off the phone within two minutes or less. (See Key Number 1 above.) Simply doing this will dramatically raise your compliance rates and the number of people who actually show up for a presentation. And the more people you get to your presentations, the more you'll bring into the business. It's that simple. If you're still on the line after the two-minute mark, you're begging, arguing, or answering too many questions.

3. Have your dream board in sight. You need to keep your passion and intensity high. And one of the great ways to do that is staying focused on why you're doing this to begin with. Your dream board is a great reminder.

4. Include your candidate's spouse or partner in the invitation. Frequently, you'll have someone attend a presentation and they're over the moon to sign up immediately. Then they go home to a skeptical spouse and drop out faster than they signed up. A couple that signs up together usually stays in the business, because one can revitalize the other in times of weakness.

5. Repeat the details of the appointment at the end of the call. You're confirming that you both heard the same thing and anchoring the appointment in their mind.

6. Never call back to reconfirm. Doing this only invites postponements and cancellations. (Sending a Google calendar invite or using a similar service can be effective, however.)

7. Schedule an exclusive block of time for making invitation calls. Block anywhere from 30 to 90 minutes just for making calls with no distractions. You'll build momentum and productivity. And you'll get enough positive responses to create traction for your events.

8. Answer a question with another question. At the actual presentations, I always want you to answer every question directly. However, in the invitation process, remember—the candidate doesn't know what he doesn't know. You need to keep enough intrigue in play to ensure that if they're a viable candidate, they will get a chance to see the presentation. (So they have enough information to make the best decision for themselves.) You can do this best by answering every question with another question. I'll give you some examples below.

9. Customize your invitation to their wants. Any time you have knowledge of what someone wants in their life, you have an opportunity to customize the invitation and increase its effectiveness. If you're close with someone, they might have mentioned something like wishing to pay down their credit card debt, finance their kid's foreign exchange trip, or build a swimming pool in their yard. You have the chance to intrigue them with the possibility that what they are about to see might help them realize their aspiration.

10. Never end on a bad call. If you get a jerk, or just someone who is cynical and negative, you can't stop there. (Otherwise, you might fall into a procrastination path for the future.) If you find yourself on a negative call, get off it quickly and punch the next number on your list immediately. If that call goes great, you might be more motivated to make another and another. Let the positive energy feed on itself.

Actual Invitation Templates

Allow me to share with you some of the most successful invitation templates I've used. If you're new, or having trouble getting people to respond to your invitations, these will help you a great deal. The key here is using these templates as a guide to see what kind of approach works best for you. But keep this mind: A relaxed, natural invitation—even if it isn't perfect—will always outperform a perfectly scripted invitation that you are obviously reading. Look through these suggestions, find one that matches your vibe, and then tweak it to your style and personality. I've broken them down into categories for different scenarios.

Inviting to a Live Event   This first approach is one you can use to invite people to physical meetings, whether they are one-on-ones, home get-togethers, or hotel events.

First thing to ask: *"You got a couple minutes?"* You need to make sure they're not in the middle of something urgent. If they are, let them know you'll call back and get off the phone.

If they do have a couple minutes, ask, *"What are you doing Tuesday night?"* If they say they're out of town, working, or busy, get off the phone quickly without giving away why you called. They'll ask why, but just tell them you wanted to do something with them and will try another time. (Or if you're going for a one-on-one, or have another possible meeting time, then say, *"What about Thursday then?"*)

Of course, most of the time the answer is "Nothing" or "Watching television." Then you go with the actual invite. Remember some of the key tips I gave you above: Get off the phone in less than two minutes. Don't get dragged into an interrogation. Answer their questions with a question.

Say something like, *"I'm hosting a presentation on creating residual income, and I'd like to invite you as my guest."* Or, *"I'm going to a presentation on creating residual income, and I'd like to bring you as my guest."*

It's just human nature that they will ask you what the presentation is. You give them one answer, free. Say something like, *"It's a presentation on building cash flow. Wanna come?"*

That leads you to the response part of the process. You're looking for people who are looking. So the invite is not about selling, begging, or convincing. Now you go into a "three strikes and you're out" mindset.

Someone who is definitely looking will say yes. If so, confirm the place and time, and jump off the call. Make your next call while you're feeling frisky. However, most people will try and start the interrogation here. They usually say something like:

But what is it?

Is this ABC company?

Is this one of those MLM things?

What kind of business is it?

What's the name of the company?

That's strike one. And no matter what they say, you respond with a question: *"Have you read any of Robert Kiyosaki's* Rich Dad, Poor Dad *books? You'll understand perfectly when you see the presentation. Can you come?"*

Or, *"Yes, it is ABC company. What do you know about it?"* Let them answer—the answer almost doesn't matter—and say, *"Great, a lot has changed about the company and you should see it all. Can you make it?"*

Or, *"No, it's not what you're calling MLM. This is an evolution of the business called Leveraged Sales. What do you know about it?"* Let them answer—again, the answer almost doesn't matter – and say, *"Great, a lot has changed about it and you should see it all. Can you make it?"*

If they say yes, confirm the place and time, and bounce. Make your next call while you're hot.

Some will still ask questions:

That's strike two. And no matter what they say, you respond with a question: *"Have you read Randy Gage's book* Mad Genius? *You'll understand it perfectly when you see the presentation. Can you come?"*

If they say yes, confirm the place and time, and get off the phone. Make your next call while you're hot.

If they say no or ask more questions again, that's strike three. You say, *"Doesn't sound like you're looking right now, so let's forget it. Let me know if you change your mind."*

Then get off the call and on to your next one. Don't beg, don't bargain, and don't diminish the opportunity. If they're not looking, you're not looking for them. For some people, this "takeaway" is what actually gets them to say yes.

You want to be able to set aside enough time for invitations so you can get in at least 20 or 30 calls. This way you're not emotionally invested in everyone saying yes. You're making enough invites to get some serious traction for your event. Maintain your passion, intensity, and urgency. Look for the people who respond to your excitement, and get off the phone quickly with those who don't.

Phone Invitations to View an Online Presentation   Now let's discuss how you can handle candidates when you're not inviting them to a physical presentation but asking them to look over a tool or watch a streaming presentation...

To have a successful Major Blast, you want to get at least 50 to 60 people from your list watching a presentation in your first 10 days (average five per day). Not everyone will review it immediately, of course, but you want to get at least 25 to 30 high-quality exposures from this. (Meaning people who will actually take the time to watch the presentation.) This could be a video hosted somewhere or a link to your replicated website. (You can also modify these slightly to invite people to live online presentations.)

This is my suggested "go-to" approach for people you can't get to a live presentation because (1) they live too far away or (2) you don't have strong influence with them. This also works great when you have a short preview or intrigue video to gauge candidates' interest.

"Hey [Name]! What are you doing right this second? I'm going to text you a link to a video. Will you take 20 minutes right now, watch it, and call me back as soon as you're done?"

"Hey [Name]! As soon as we hang up, I'm going to text you a link to a video. Will you take three minutes to watch it and call me as soon as you're done?"

"Hey [Name]! Can you grab a pen please? Write down this website: [URL] It's about a new business I'm launching and I'd love your take on it. Please take a look, and I'll call you back in 20 minutes to talk about it."

"Hi [Name], I'm launching something hot, and you're one of the first people I thought of. I believe you could do well with this. Have you got a pen? Please go to [website] and check this out. I'm trying to earn a new BMW and I think you can too. Check it out, and I'll call you back at [time] to talk to you about it."

"Hi [Name], I'm putting together a group of the brightest people I know to launch a new project. Your skillset seems perfect for it. If I text you a link, would you take 20 minutes and watch this online presentation for me?"

As always, create a sense of anticipation on their part and get off the phone quickly. Don't get drawn into a bunch of questions.

Text/Email Inviting to an Online Presentation This approach is perfect for the people with whom you don't have strong influence or haven't had contact in a while. Oftentimes these are old schoolmates, former neighbors, and others on your holiday card list. Or people you have only emails for. It can also be used for connections in online groups.

It's a simple two-step qualifying process. The first message ascertains whether they have any interest, and the second one directs them to a website or online presentation.

I did amazingly well with this process when I relaunched my business. It allowed me to spend time with the people who showed a genuine interest and not waste time with people who weren't good candidates. In the following examples, you'll notice that I was right up front that this was Direct Selling. If they had a problem with that, I didn't want to squander my time or theirs.

You're welcome to use this example as is or work with your sponsorship line to create a template email that is specific to your company.

Message One

SUBJECT LINE: Residual Income Biz

Hi [Name],

Are you interested in looking at a side business that can generate a very serious residual income? I'm launching something huge, and I'd love to have you on my team.

I am working with an emerging Direct Selling company that meets the criteria to blow up in a big way. Things are starting to take off, and I'm looking for leaders in your area. We're seeking people with good teaching and training skills who want to capitalize on a chance to get in early.

Here are the factors that make this such a powerful opportunity right now:

1. **You Can Be in From the Beginning**
   The company has recently launched in [country]. So we have a real window of opportunity to get ahead in the race before most people even know there is one. We're looking for leaders we can train in our team system to own their local market and springboard from there.

2. **Serious Residual Income Available**

   I'm sure you're aware how important it is to have residual income to create true wealth. With this business, the compensation plan offers seven ways to earn, with most of them residual.

3. **Products People Crave**

   There are many lifestyle factors and trends that make these products in serious demand. This ensures you a stable business and income for many years to come.

   So do you want to hear about this? Or are you too busy with your other stuff to look?

   Please get back with me right away.

   Thanks,

   [Your Name]

Message Two

Hi [Name],

Glad we had a chance to connect and that you're interested. I believe you can do great with this because of who you are.

We have set up a very simple system that anyone can duplicate. Please go to [link] and review the information. Then let's talk just as soon as you're done. We're moving fast right now and I'd love to have you on my team.

Thanks,

[Your Name]

Note: Just like the phone invitations, if you customize each message with a few personal comments, your response rate will be higher. *Also, these should be sent only to people that you know!* They won't work well with strangers, and you would be leaving yourself open to spam regulations if you send it to rented lists.

You'll also probably get thrown out of online groups if you bulk send to everybody.

Follow up within 24 hours for best results. If your candidate is interested, but not ready to join, escalate the process. This can be done by doing a follow-up video, setting up a three-way call with your sponsor, sending your candidate to an opportunity meeting in their area, or getting them on a ZOOM or Skype call.

Inviting When You've Got One Shot

Here's an approach for when you run into someone who impresses you, but you might never see them again. (It could be a helpful retail clerk, a courteous Lyft or Uber driver, or an extra-friendly flight attendant.) Look through these ideas and see which ones feel right for you.

> "[Name], you're really impressive at what you do. You would be marvelous at my business. If I send a link to your phone, would you being willing to watch an 11-minute video?"

> "You know, you are way too good doing what you do—to be doing what you do. I bet you would be amazing in my business. If I send you a link, would you be willing to review a short video and let me know what you think?"

> "[Name], I'm very impressed at the job you do here. I believe you would be very successful in the business I'm in. If I send you a link, would you be willing to review a short video and let me know what you think?"

> "You know I am very impressed at the job you do here. Are you familiar with Direct Selling? I'm in an [emerging/new/expanding/established] company that is looking for leaders. If I send you a link, would you be willing to review a short video and let me know what you think?"

"[Name], I'm a big believer in income diversification, and I have launched a new business to accomplish that. My guess is that you will be more than intrigued with the info on this flash drive. If I give it to you, would you be willing to review the video presentation it holds and let me know what you think?"

"[Name], I'm a big believer in income diversification, and I have launched a new business to accomplish that. My guess is that you will be more than intrigued with the info in this magazine. If I give it to you, would you be willing to read it and let me know what you think?"

Here was my best go-to strategy when (cue Eminem from *8 Mile*), "But you only got one shot, Gotta give me all you got..."

I haven't used a business card in almost 15 years. But I created a sexy card to hand out in those situations when you have just one shot with someone. I get mine from MOO Cards (https://www.moo.com), but you can have them made other places, I'm sure. With MOO, I get the "Luxe" version, which is extra-thick, superfine Mohawk paper with a colored seam and textured finish. I have a few lines of intriguing copy, along with my name and contact info, but the real focus is the link to my replicated website featuring the recruiting video.

So if I meet an Uber driver who really impresses me, I use one of the approaches above, then simply give them the card (and leave a generous tip). If they are a serious candidate, they watch the presentation. If they aren't really looking for something, they don't watch. And I never give it another thought unless I hear from them. (You might get better results if you get their phone number and follow up after, but that's not my style.)

* * *

In all the cases above, you will have much more compliance with people reviewing the materials and a better response if you distribute them with a sense of urgency. Use an energetic and busy approach, but don't go overboard trying to pressure the candidate. Let them know that you are moving fast and ask for their commitment to review the materials quickly. If they really don't seem interested to look at the information, thank them for their time and move on.

Especially for the people in your warm market, your best results will come when you qualify your candidate and organize a time to get back with them. Here's what that will look like:

> After your candidate agrees to review the information, say, *"Great! When do you think you can see it for sure?"* Wait for their response. What time they give you is unimportant. Then say, *"So, if I call you [right after they said they'd see it], you'll have seen it for sure, right?"* After they confirm this, ask for the best number to call them.

This way, the candidate has had several opportunities to say they'll watch it and by using this commitment approach (and if you have the proper posture), you will have a 70 or 80 percent compliance rate. (And better duplication throughout your organization.) Without it, you will have a much lower rate or worse duplication throughout your organization.

> When you follow up as you agreed you would, you simply ask, *"Did you have a chance to review the information?"*

> If they tell you they have not reviewed the presentation yet, say something like, *"It's really important. When do you think you could see it for sure for sure?"* Wait for their answer and say, *"Great, so if I call you on [new time you set], you'll have seen it for sure?"*

Just keep repeating this process until they actually review the presentation or tell you they are not interested.

A Few Key Thoughts to Revisit

Some of your best leaders will likely come from people you don't know yet. So as you go through your day, be on the lookout for sharp people. People who are successful in others areas usually are successful in Direct Selling too. Keep honing your skills on meeting people.

Sometimes you get only that one shot. So always have some of your prospecting tools in your car, purse, or briefcase for when you meet a great candidate.

Inviting is the money skill. Like I said earlier, it's the most lucrative skill you can develop. Use these templates, test them, and modify these approaches to fit your natural personality. It's a good idea to even role-play with someone in your sponsorship line. They'll have insights on how you can customize them to your opportunity to make them even more effective.

The better you get at inviting, the more qualified candidates you'll have attending your live presentations. And the more qualified candidates you get in front of a presentation, the more new enrollments you will have. Which is exactly what we'll work on next...

CHAPTER 8

The Science of Successful Recruiting

The basis for creating wealth in Leveraged Sales is facilitating duplication down the group. To do that, you have to follow the formula we discussed earlier:

> *Empower a large group of people to perform a few simple actions on an ongoing basis.*

Launching your business with a Major Blast helps you begin this formula the right way, because you're getting enough traction to create the "large group of people" requirement. Anyone with any level of experience or education can follow these simple steps. And you will notice that all of these involve using third-party resources. This makes sure that the business is not about you and that anyone can duplicate your results.

Examples of third-party tools would be product catalogs and brochures, a booklet explaining the comp plan, videos, audios, replicated websites, a presentation flipchart, or online presentations. Even product samples and a testimonial from someone on a three-way call would qualify as third-party tools. Believe it or not, having extra copies of this book can be a powerfully effective third-party follow-up tool. You certainly wouldn't give it to everyone. But when you have a serious candidate and they express a genuine desire to understand the business before they join, this book can educate them to the huge potential the business offers.

It's not an accident that the word "science" is in this chapter's title. Because there really is a science to presenting the business in a manner that causes the appropriate people to join your team.

Scientists propose hypotheses to explain theories, and then design studies to test those hypotheses. The steps must be repeatable (duplicable) to dependably predict future results. They take those theories and bind them together into a coherent structure. That's what you will find here. My step-by-step system for building a large, exponentially growing network of distributors.

And like all science, this system must be based on observable, empirical, and measurable evidence. *Repeatable results.* The evidence I introduce to you here has been subject to specific principles of reasoning and demonstrated by relentless observation and experimentation.

You are able to create those "repeatable results" by always following a standard system and using third-party resources. That way, the presentations aren't about you, but the team, system, and opportunity. Trust the process. Be sure to schedule specific follow-up times when you give someone a tool. If there is any interest (even if they have questions), then immediately escalate them to another level by booking the next appointment or giving them a follow-up tool.

The key to all of this is getting sufficient people evaluating your business. As you go about it, maintain a strong posture. Be in a hurry. *You* have the gift. Don't ever beg. Don't be emotionally attached to the outcome with your candidate. And if they don't like it, they will be rejecting the tool, not you.

Before going further, let's talk more about this concept of using third-party tools. These are critical, because, as we discussed earlier, using a tool removes you from the equation. (Which is necessary to create true duplication.) That way, if you just started two days ago and haven't made a penny yet, no candidates will hold that against you. And if you're an experienced professional raking in $100K a month, no one will think they can't match those results and hold that against you either. Using tools ensures that neither your strengths or weaknesses nor your experience or lack of it are used against you to diminish your duplication.

Think of this practice as the triangle principle. It should never be a two-way interaction between just you and the candidate. You want a three-way triangle: you, the candidate, and a tool.

Note: Please understand that what I am sharing with you here (and all throughout the book) are guidelines. I'm sharing what worked for me, my team, and my consulting clients. *But you should check everything with your sponsorship line.* Because they will have specifics and nuances that you should be cognizant of.

Back in Chapter 4, I shared with you the key elements of a Major Blast. Let's look at that list again:

- A social get-together for obtaining your initial customer base.
- Two or three presentations to launch in your local market.
- An electronic campaign through email, SMS, and messaging apps.
- Distribution of mass-market recruiting materials in appropriate places.
- Editing or creating your social media accounts to promote your business.
- Moving people from all of these funnels "up the ladder" to bigger presentations (online and offline).

You have already learned how to do the social get-together for potential customers in Chapter 6. Now let's look at your two or three launch presentations. I'm going to go old school here and suggest you do these at your home. (Including and especially if your home is a small studio apartment, mobile home, or even under a staircase at 4 Privet Drive.)

CONDUCTING HOME MEETINGS

You'll hear from some people that home meetings are no longer effective. They are certainly entitled to their opinion, but the facts don't support that. People who say home meetings don't work don't do home meetings. But people who are actually *doing* home meetings will testify that they are still extremely effective.

There are gurus and marketers suggesting that you can build the business by talking only to strangers, pitching groups on Facebook, or renting email lists. Those "stay home in your Chewbacca pajamas" strategies don't duplicate longterm. And they're ridiculous in the sense that many of them actually suggest you shouldn't talk to your friends, neighbors, and acquaintances. If the people promoting these strategies really believed in our profession, they'd be talking to the people they care about. Most of them are not actually in our business; they make their money selling theoretical advice to people who are.

So if you want to say you hate home meetings and don't want to do them, no one is going to force you to do otherwise. But please don't say it's because meetings are ineffective. Because today they're more successful than ever.

In my team, we dubbed these home events "Private Business Receptions" (PBRs), but you can call them anything you want. These are informal get-togethers where you can invite the key people you would like to have on your team to preview the opportunity. Ideally, you want to have a video for the presentation or someone from your sponsorship line doing a presentation for you. (For duplication purposes.) This is a very friendly, nonthreatening way for candidates to see what the business is all about.

Your goal is to host two or three PBRs in your first 7 to 10 days. Having a series of meetings like this will allow more of your candidates the flexibility to find a date that works for them. It also ensures that you enroll enough distributors to uncover a few serious people who will run with the business in a big way.

You can expect some pushback from new team members who don't want to do home events and believe everything can be handled online. But they will miss a great opportunity with that belief. Home presentations are very palatable to candidates, because they involve simply stopping by a friend's house. And they are very duplicable. Especially if you keep them short, fun, and social, instead of long, boring, and stringent.

Here are some guidelines to conducting the most effective PBRs and getting off to a fast start:

Prior to the PBR

- Look over your candidate list to determine your best candidates and invite them to your home. Let them know you are having the "Grand Opening" of your new business and want them there to support you and see what it is all about.

- Don't get drawn into a lot of questions. If they ask, let them know the name of the company and that you have a special video or streaming presentation you want them to see, or someone you want them to meet. Explain that you are brand new yourself, but the presentation will provide the answers they are seeking. Follow the same advice I gave you on this in Chapter 7.

- Remove all distractions before the presentation (phone, pets, children, etc.).

- Do not set up the furniture in the home for a meeting. Keep everything normal, and move chairs in or around when necessary as people arrive.

- Provide only beverages (no alcohol) or light snacks. (Don't show off your legendary culinary skills, because most people can't duplicate that.)

- Have packets prepared for each guest, but keep them out of sight.

- Don't set up a product display. (That distracts people and kills the presentation flow.)

The PBR Itself

- Welcome people as they arrive and seat them comfortably. Introduce guests to each other and start some friendly social conversation.

- Start within a few minutes of the scheduled time. Do not talk about people who are late or did not show. Concentrate on those who are there.

- To begin, welcome everyone officially and thank them for attending. Give a 30-second testimonial for why you're in the business, then play the video or introduce the speaker. (Edify the video or speaker. Promote, don't just announce. People should be able to tell that you're excited about this.)

- It's a good idea to lay out the structure of the meeting to the attendees, so people know what they are going to experience and how long it will last. Eliminate the mystery so that they can relax.

- Don't be running around the house during the presentation. Stay seated and watch the presentation with your guests.

- If others arrive late, don't start over. Let them know that you will catch them up later privately.

- When the presentation finishes, hand out the info packets for each guest.

Now is the time to answer questions. If your sponsor is there, calling in, or coming in via the Internet, let them handle these. If your sponsor is not there, use the tools for answers. Example: If there are questions about the compensation plan, direct candidates to the appropriate sections in the literature. If there are product questions, use the catalog.

If you don't have a tool for the answer and don't know it yourself, learn to say, "I don't know. But I will find the answer and get back to you." There's nothing wrong with that, so say it with posture. People will then know that they can start this without being perfect and knowing everything.

When you see someone is quite interested, ask if they get it. (Literally, I say, "Do you get this?") If they respond positively, then ask if they are ready to get started. Sign up those who say yes. Schedule their new member orientation right then.

For those who do not sign up, invite them to review the info pack. Let them know that you are building fast and want them to look over the materials promptly to make sure they capitalize on the opportunity. (No hard sell. But definitely a posture of passion, intensity, and urgency.) Schedule a follow-up call, or if there is another PBR or opportunity meeting coming up within a few days, invite them to that. *The most important part of any meeting is scheduling the next meeting.*

Following the PBR

- Follow up within 12 to 24 hours. Invite them again to another meeting or put them on a three-way call or webcast.

- Help your new team members schedule their own PBR series and start duplicating the process!

A few things to create a successful experience: Start on time and be brief. Don't over-talk the business. Let the tools do the work. Be professional but not stilted. Don't change your personality. Be you—the professional version of you.

CONDUCTING ONE-ON-ONES

Another offshoot option on this is doing small, informal one-on-one presentations between you and a candidate. There are some people and situations where these are appropriate. Here are some tips for those.

Like every other kind of presentation, third-party tools are key. If you just meet someone for a one-on-one and you make an impassioned, astonishing presentation pouring out your heart and soul—you'll probably sign them up. But you won't have much duplication.

When you're training a new team member, you might help them by doing some two-on-ones with them. But do that only as long as needed. Push them out of the nest to do their own one-on-ones.

Don't "gang up" when conducting two-on-ones. If your sponsor is the one leading the presentation, defer to her. If the second person starts chiming in, the candidate might feel a two-against-one dynamic and become defensive. (Of course, two-on-ones can also be done with phone, ZOOM, and Skype calls.)

At the same time you're setting up your initial PBRs and one-on-ones, you want to be conducting your electronic campaign through email, text, and messaging apps. (Follow the steps outlined in Chapter 7.)

You should also be editing your social media profiles to promote your new business and begin approaching key people on those platforms. Don't go over the top here with a hard sell. You don't want people doing searches on your product or company before you've even had a chance to chat with them. Simply create curiosity. We'll look at the specifics of that more in Chapter 9.

Now let's look at the next part of the process—moving people from all of these funnels "up the ladder" to bigger presentations. Use these large meetings for the final stages in the ladder of escalation process. Candidates you bring at this point should be prequalified, having already seen some type of smaller presentation.

FOR LARGE-VENUE PRESENTATIONS

My thinking on large hotel opportunity meetings has evolved a great deal over the past 10 years. I will discuss that in depth shortly. For now, let's talk about the logistics of the process.

If the meeting is to be held in a public location, selecting the site is important. Hotel meeting rooms are usually the best, because they are conveniently located, nonthreatening, and have adequate parking and other facilities you need.

Your candidate will judge your program by the caliber of the surroundings in which it is presented. Everything you present to the candidate should be professional. Choose a mid-level property. The Ritz Carlton, Mandarin Oriental, and Four Seasons are too pricey, and parking fees alone may be $60. Avoid downscale places like Holiday Inns and other motels. Marriott, Hilton, and Sheraton usually work well. And the spinoff brands from those chains often have the best value for meeting rooms. Courtyard by Marriott, Springhill Suites, and Hilton Garden Inn usually have meeting rooms but don't expect or require you to also purchase meals and catering.

Visit the hotel in person and look at your potential meeting room. Make sure the carpet, wallpaper, and decor are light and attractive. Avoid rooms with a baroque, dark mahogany-type decor. Don't book a room with pillars that obstruct view. Make sure the ceiling is at least 10 feet high. It's tough to be grand in a low-ceilinged room.

Check the parking rates, as high parking fees will discourage guests. Check the prices for microphones, screens, and other audio-visual materials you plan to use. Most hotels farm out these services to outside vendors, so they are not negotiable. Sometimes these costs are more than the room rent. In many cases, it's cheaper to buy your own. Some hotels, knowing you need a screen or a whiteboard, will charge you $150, even though that screen or board is built into the wall of the room.

What is negotiable? The room rent. Never pay the price first quoted you. These prices are only for neophytes who don't know any better. Inform the hotel that you will be renting rooms regularly. If the price quoted you is $400, tell them your budget is only $150 and ask what they have in that range. Often they will then find you a meeting room for about $200. (It's actually the same room they were going to charge you $400 for.) If you hold regular meetings, it is sometimes possible to pay only $100 or $150 for a room that lists for $500.

Note: All the previous advice here on venues is from the perspective of first-world markets. If you're building in third-world and developing countries, you have to adapt. In those places, Ritz Carlton and Four Seasons don't even exist. What are considered mid-level properties in the first world are the high-end ones in these countries. Instead of parking prices, your concern might be whether the property is near a metro line or bus stop, because most of your attendees don't have cars. *Adjust accordingly to the markets you are building in.*

Room Setup

Now let's look at the room setup. If possible, put the lectern and screen on a raised platform. It gives the speaker more credibility and provides better visibility for the guests. Just as with home meetings, make sure it is at the opposite end of the room from the door, so late arrivals won't disrupt the presentation for others.

If you're using video or PowerPoint, don't place the screen behind the speaker. They can't see the audience because the projector is shining in their eyes, and the audience can't see the screen because there is a human being located in front of it. Set the screen off to the side.

When I wrote my first book, I recommended that you have a large banner or sign with your company's name at the front of the room. I also suggested having an attractive product display table and perhaps a "prosperity" table. (This is like the product table, but it features car brochures, pictures of local people winning awards, travel brochures, etc. If your company has award programs, a President's Club, etc., you would have those brochures on this table.)

I began to see the meetings getting grander and grander. It got to the point that each city I visited to do meetings had a bigger, better setup than the last one. People were making photo boards, collages, and banners, hanging bunting, generally making the meeting rooms gorgeous. They were racing from work at 5 p.m. to have their rooms decorated by 8 o'clock. They stopped thinking about getting candidates there because they were concentrating so much on the room setup. So look for some balance here. We want a sharp room, but it's all about packing that room with guests.

Other Setup Notes

Set out chairs for only three quarters of the people you expect. Have extras in the service hallway where they can be brought in quickly, but don't set them out. *Once the meeting is about to start, there should never be a naked chair.* The more crowded your room is, the more likely it is that candidates will join. It's better to be in a smaller room with people standing around the walls, than in a large room with empty seats.

Have one or two volunteers who arrive early enough to thoroughly check all the audiovisual equipment. Have extra projector bulbs, and so on, and check all the volume levels, including the microphone. Have the necessary adapters for your laptop or smartphone and a playlist of up-tempo music. The hotel will assure you that they have all the necessary dongles, extra bulbs, fresh batteries, and so on. They will be lying.

One hour before meeting time, set the room thermostat to 65°F (18°C). It needs to be this cool so that when the guests fill up the room, the temperature will remain bearable. If the room is not kept at a proper temperature, the meeting will suffer. The same can be said for lighting. Make sure the room is brightly lit.

Set up the registration table in the hallway so late arrivals won't disrupt the other people. Encourage all distributors to wear their rank or other achievement pins. Pick your friendliest, most positive people for the greeter, registration, and door positions.

Have the music playing for 30 minutes prior to the meeting. Gradually raise the volume as the room fills to dial up the energy in the room. Have uplifting music ready to start immediately at the conclusion of the meeting. Studies have shown that the right music increases consumer purchases as much as 15 percent.

Meetings should be fast-paced, intriguing, informational, professional, and *fun!* The smaller home meetings feed the larger hotel meetings. Having this structure in place allows distributors to bring their candidates through the gradually escalating process we talked about in earlier chapters

Notice that up until now, we haven't even discussed the actual meeting. Because... all of these things you do before the meeting are just as important as the meeting itself. Little things are everything.

The Meeting Itself

Begin by starting on time. If your meeting is scheduled for 7:30 p.m., it should start then, but certainly no later than 7:35. If you wait for late people, you will set a precedent and have to start later and later every time. In reality, the people who are likely to sponsor in and do the business successfully are the ones who arrive at functions on time.

It may sound strange, but you actually have to train your people how to go to meetings. Teach them that the real meetings are the ones that take place before and after the regular meeting.

If you want to be certain a candidate is coming to the meeting, pick him up. You can say something like, "If it's okay, I'll pick you up and we can talk on the way."

Get your guest to the meeting 15 to 20 minutes early so you can get seats in the front rows. The closer a guest is to the speaker, the more the guest will be impacted. This also gives you a chance to introduce your guest around. Let them meet your sponsor, any high-level pin ranks in the room, and any other distributors with commonalities (same organization, same occupation, etc.). And definitely be sure to introduce them to that night's speaker. Now, instead of seeing the speaker as a stranger trying to sell them something—the candidate will be listening to what their new friend they just met has to impart.

Other things you'll have to teach your distributors about attending meetings:

- It is important to attend every meeting, whether or not they have a guest.
- Be generous with applause and laughter.
- No food, gum, or drinks during the meeting.
- Don't be texting or playing games on their cell. Watch the presenter.
- Participate if the speaker calls for it, particularly during the dream building, as candidates may be very hesitant to get involved in this.

After the meeting, you will want to keep the discussion centered on the business. Answer any questions your candidate has, and see if they're ready to join. If not, go through the pack of materials you're sending home with them and schedule the next meeting.

Meetings definitely require work, and they take continuous effort. But the rewards are too powerful to ignore. You can find some teams that promote their opportunities as "no meetings required." Here's what I know. In the more than 60-year history of Direct Selling, no company has ever hit the exponential growth curve—and continued to prosper thereafter—without holding meetings.

CONDUCTING ONLINE PRESENTATIONS

That takes us to the debate of whether meetings should be online or offline. The correct answer is yes.

Truth is, a large percentage of the meetings that used to be conducted in hotels are now being streamed live on the Internet instead. And I love this development. The online presentations can be an even bigger stage, provide even more social proof, and recruit even more people.

The basic dynamics of what happens for the online meetings are pretty much the same as the offline ones in terms of content and what should happen afterward. My advice to you is don't go for one or the other. Integrate the two mediums to achieve the most powerful results.

If you are doing the first stages of the Major Blast correctly, you'll always have people coming to the bigger meetings. And if you manage the meetings the right way, people will enjoy and look forward to attending.

There are different schools of thought on the content of the presentations at the top of the ladder. There are arguments to be made for two models, and I'd like to share both with you. (And then I'll reveal my own personal practice afterward.)

Option 1: Traditional Meeting

Option one is the traditional opportunity meeting. This scenario has been working effectively for about six decades. You cover all of the segments important to a candidate evaluating the business. These include:

- Lifestyle benefits
- Product line benefits for consumers
- The demand for and marketability of the product line for builders
- The power of leverage
- How the candidate can harness that leverage and earn in the plan
- What the culture of your company is, and why someone would want to be associated with it
- The support structure and system in place to help people be successful
- The importance of timing and positioning
- A call to action

Option 2: Weekly Leadership School

The second option is one used with great success by Luca Melloni and his wife, Lily Rosales. Instead of a traditional opportunity presentation, their team conducts weekly leadership schools. (This is an idea I gave them many years ago, and—to my great shame and humiliation—they implemented it much better than I ever did!)

The leadership school agenda is divided into three parts: product training, skillset training, and the final segment where someone shares their success story.

Each of these segments is presented by a different person. They do them as training and are critiqued and coached the following day by a leadership committee. *The most intriguing part about all this is how it is presented to the candidate.* (It's an approach I have used with great success.)

The candidates are told that they are coming to a training event, not a presentation. You let them know that no one will be trying to sell them anything—so they can relax and just see for themselves how the business is actually done. And after seeing how it works, they can decide if the business is right for them. Candidates are much less defensive in this scenario. Yet they still get presented some great content that can compel them to join the business.

Now let's discuss the issue of whether to conduct opportunity presentations or hold training schools…

My Preference

I prefer the leadership school approach. But when I'm launching a new company—or in a new country for an existing company—I find that 6 to 12 months of opportunity presentations (online and offline) create the kind of fervent kinetic action I'm looking for.

One dynamic is the same for both options: These should not be the first time a candidate is hearing about the opportunity. A presentation at this level should be attended only by someone who has had at least one or two impressions already, and this step is another rung up on the ladder of escalation.

Another dynamic that is the same for either option is that the most important meeting is the meeting after the meeting. You need to give the candidate the appropriate marketing materials and answer any questions they have. Take a pulse as to whether they're ready to join, and if so, get them enrolled. If they're not ready, keep moving them up the ladder.

Most people don't join the first or even second time they see the business. And often, not at the presentations, but during the followup afterward. It is only as you pull them up the ladder of escalation that they make that decision. Keep checking back with your candidates and moving them to the next rung in the ladder until they join or tell you that have decided it isn't right for them. Followup is where most of the action happens.

Some distributors feel that it's the company's place to conduct and pay for meetings. This couldn't be further from the truth. Remember, this is *your* business and *your* bonus check. It is the field leaders' responsibility to set up and hold meetings, and paying for them is just part of the normal investment in running your business. (Although new companies often sponsor meetings for the first few months after launching.)

The concept of holding meetings to generate interest in a business or product worked in 1970, 1990, 2010, and it will still be working in 2030. If you want the long-term security that comes from building depth—there's no better way than the proper meeting structure.

Note: I've given you the logistics for all the different types of meetings and presentations. Different companies have different models. Please consult with your sponsorship line to learn what process they are using.

SUPPORTING YOUR RETAILERS

Before we move on, we need to address the issue of distributors who want to retail but aren't interested in building a team. (I didn't write this book for them. This would be information overload for them. I'm bringing up the subject here so you know how to best support the people on your team who choose this option.)

Your retailers are most excited about the products and want to concentrate on marketing them. They won't want the regular new member orientation, aren't going to attend opportunity meetings, and won't do a Major Blast, so don't try to push them into one. Their only desire is to use the products themselves and retail the products to friends.

So instead of pressuring them to attend the builder events—simply spend an hour or two when you sign them up explaining the information that is relevant to them: Procedures such as how to order products, sign up autoship customers, and the refund. (For the best duplication, develop a standardized new retailer orientation.)

Keep your retailers informed about the event schedule, let them know that they're always welcome, but don't pressure them to attend everything. Advise them that you're always available when they have questions or need help.

Also let them know that it's likely they will encounter people who want to be builders (sponsoring and duplicating). Advise them to bring these people to you. Business builders are going to need help with presentations, training, counseling, and other group-building functions that a retailer sponsor cannot give them. When you get a builder under a retailer, you will work with the builder as though they were on your first level.

Note: When this happens, it would be wise for you to suggest that the retailer may want to reconsider becoming a builder. They are already doing most of the things required. By adding a few more presentations, they could upgrade to the builder model and receive even greater rewards. Inevitably, retailers will stumble across people who want to build a big business, and they will leave a lot of money on the table if they don't upgrade at some point. But don't pressure them. If they desire to remain retailers, be grateful for them and support their decision.

BONUS TIPS ON PRESENTING AND ENROLLING
Bonus Tip Number One

No one in a legitimate opportunity ever felt the need to utter the words, "This is 100 percent legal." In fact, the only times I've ever heard anyone speak those words it was because what they were promoting was a hot, sketchy mess.

Bonus Tip Number Two

Presenting is one of those areas where activity can actually overcome skill. A person who gets busy organizing many candidates in front of presentations—even if their inviting skills are still a work in progress—will always out-earn someone sitting at home trying to develop the perfect invitation. The person who gets the most candidates in front of a presentation wins.

Bonus Tip Number Three

Statistics tell. Stories sell. There are not a lot of people who are inspired to do something because of a statistic someone quotes them. Make sure all your presentations—in all forms—utilize the power of storytelling.

Bonus Tip Number Four

Don't close people. Open them. Remember that true duplication will never occur if your business is built on high-pressure closing and manipulation techniques. Your job is to educate your candidates. Give them enough information to make the best decision for them, not you.

Bonus Tip Number Five

Sponsor your weakness. If you really understand this tip, it's worth a fortune to you. The truly delicious thing about our business is that you can neutralize any weakness you have by sponsoring someone who counteracts that limitation.

Are you pathologically shy the way I was? Sponsor people who are gregarious. Don't have much money to work the business? Sponsor someone who does. Don't have a car to get to meetings? Sponsor someone with a car.

It's the jiu-jitsu of duplication.

Next, we're going to investigate how you can harness social media to grow your business…

CHAPTER 9

Harnessing E-Commerce and Social Media to Explode Growth

I got a WhatsApp message from Art Jonak. The title alone had me petrified to click:

"MLMers on Instagram versus MLMers in Real Life."

I could only imagine what the link would reveal... The posers and imposters who rent a Ferrari for a day, posting pix like they own it; the beginners earning $400 a month that claim to be millionaires; or would it be a guy with a beer in one hand and a cigarette in the other, promoting a wellness company?

I held my breath and clicked...

False alarm! Fortunately, the post turned out to be a clever Instagram account from a comedienne just poking fun at people's social media exaggerations in general.

But my trepidation when I saw the first message was real. Very, very real. How many times have we held our breath, or our nose, as we watched someone promoting our business as they stray over the line of integrity?

It's a whole new world. Now the situation isn't just some guy bloviating to five people in his living room, or even a sketchy team member exaggerating in front of 200 people in a Marriott conference room. There are people making posts on social media that sometimes get thousands, tens of thousands, or even millions of views. Your events are being live-streamed across the Internet. And there is a digital record of every stupid, ignorant, or illegal claim your people ever make.

So how do we make this problem go away?

We don't. So let's get that out of the way right now. Boo.

The dark side of technology is like bullying, child abuse, and mistreating animals. You can hate these problems, speak out about them, and fight them. (And you should.) But unless you remove humans from the equation, these issues will always exist. So company executives—and even many team leaders—might not like what I have to say next, but it's the truth.

The Internet is not a fad, and you can't keep waiting for it to blow over. You can't ban your people from using social media. Technology is making a cataclysmic change in the way we have to do business, and you can't stop it.

You certainly won't be able stop your people from making mistakes and sometimes crossing over the line. And the new reality of technology amplifies and exposes those mistakes to the whole planet. So we're going to have to get smarter—not just with tech in general, but with social media and e-commerce in particular.

EMBRACING E-COMMERCE, TECHNOLOGY, AND SOCIAL MEDIA

As we move away from the archaic model of hype-recruiting-based network marketing—and forward into the new model of customer-driven Leveraged Sales—I believe e-commerce, technology, and social media are the most important issues we need to address today.

When I'm consulting with executives in C-Suites these days, the advice I'm giving most frequently is:

You have to stop thinking of yourself as a [nutrition, cosmetics, utilities, skin care, cleaning products, etc.] company—and start thinking of yourself as a tech company. A tech company that happens to market [nutrition cosmetics, utilities, skin care, cleaning products, etc.].

There were about 10 of us masterminding at the home of one of the group. This was a top-secret get-together, with some of the biggest names in our profession. Jonak had put it together and dubbed it "The Billion-Dollar Retreat," because of the billions of dollars in sales produced by the teams of those attending.

We each had our chance to address the group and suggest items and issues we should devote our brainpower to. When my turn came I said the single biggest issue we faced was how we could harness tech and social media in our businesses moving forward. I challenged the group to explore what the perfect online opportunity presentation on social media would look like.

And we brainstormed that idea for two days...

Finally, we came up with a concept to test on Facebook. That was about three years ago, and the results have been stunning. Our members and many other leaders in Leveraged Sales have created huge volumes doing these kinds of presentations. And that was just the tip of the iceberg...

As a distributor, you may be intrigued with the idea of utilizing social media to build your influence. Or you might see it as a tangible strategy for growing your business. The truth is, you need to look at both aspects.

The macro is building your influence over the long term. The micro is crafting an immediate and measurable increase in your business and income right now.

Let's concentrate on the real-world reality you need to embrace. Social media is the primary method of interaction between a large percentage of our friends and family. We need to be employing this in our systems.

Social media has changed almost every personal and business interaction in the world today. Its effects are reverberating through every process of the business, from prospecting to enrolling, customer acquisition to training. As leaders, we have to immerse ourselves into integrating this into our processes, systems, and cultures immediately.

Pretty much everything that used to be done offline is today being broadcast live online. The slightest mistake with an income claim or product testimonial now has the real possibility of attracting severe regulatory action. Even a simple before-and-after pic of someone's weight loss results could be problematic in a lot of jurisdictions. Those of you operating in highly regulated industries, such as nutrition, insurance, and others, are in particular danger. I get that.

As we discussed, social media now increases the likelihood that stupid behavior will be recorded and broadcast to an audience you would rather it didn't. I get that too. But social media isn't going away any time soon. And if you don't figure out a way to effectively utilize it with your team—you and they will be at a serious marketing disadvantage.

People in our business have been predicting the death of home meetings and hotel meetings since the '80s at least. It appears those obituaries were premature, because they ain't dead yet. I would argue they never will be.

So please don't take this chapter as my argument for eliminating personal contact, warm market, and meetings. It most certainly is not that.

What I am saying is that you will employ social media even while you're working your warm market. Social media will be an integral part of the qualifying and recruiting process. And those one-on-one, home, hotel, and online presentations can and will be woven together synergistically.

And the bigger issue is the ever-increasing role technology and e-commerce are having in our business. Any company today without effective mobile apps and replicated websites is placing their distributors at a huge disadvantage.

Looking at the Potential in Growing Markets

One qualification on all this, before we dive more into specifics...

What I'm sharing with you now is the reality in first-world markets. Internet access, tech adoption, and the cost of broadband will impact the speed of implementation in markets that are currently considered second- or third-world. But this current first-world reality will eventually extend around the globe, *and much more quickly than most people realize.*

Already a large number of people doing business in poor markets, such as India and Africa, have smartphones and 3G or 4G Wi-Fi. The business model in many companies is evolving away from the old MLM style and toward an e-commerce approach more appropriate to our times. As I laid out in Chapter 2, the reputation of MLM is in tatters. But the reputation of e-commerce is sensational and getting better.

We've entered both the technology era and gig economy. People are driving Uber a few days a week, monetizing videos of their cat on YouTube, selling their handicrafts on Pinterest, and drop-shipping all sorts of things they can promote online to their friends without ever stocking any inventory.

Leveraged Sales offers a lot of e-commerce drop-ship possibilities. We need to embrace this trend and make it our own. This type of Leveraged Sales is exploding in Asia right now. People there idolize Jack Ma of Alibaba, and this is basically what he has done and teaches. And they love it.

Take a look at this tweet from Amway president Doug DeVos: "It's incredible to see how quickly mobile has changed the Amway business in China, our top market. Eighty-five percent of product sales now come from online. Great efforts by our digital leaders in China to drive a quick change across the business."

There's a mobile app called Rappi that offers an on-demand delivery service in Latin America. Users can order groceries, food, or medications—or Avon. And their products are delivered within two hours.

So not only must we embrace social media for running and promoting the business, but we need to also incorporate more aspects of e-commerce and the gig economy.

Focusing on Functionality and Processes

Because tech is changing quickly and constantly, let's not get bogged down with the intricacies of the individual platforms. They are always in a continuous state of flux. Right now Facebook and Instagram are certainly hot. A year from now it could be two completely different platforms. (And probably will be.)

So instead, I want to focus on *functionality* and *processes*. These are the critical elements in terms of how social media will be able to impact your business.

In terms of functionality, we must begin with the role of mobile apps in operating the business. In the first world, this is the biggest sea change in human behavior and marketing practices in a generation. Virtually everything we do on a daily basis is now impacted by its connection with a smartphone.

Mobile apps change how we buy, how we sell, how we connect, how we learn, and, essentially, how we do almost everything. We are fast approaching the point where there will be five billion smartphones on the planet. And no one knows how many smartwatches, other Wi-Fi gear, or even implant devices will be in use.

You're probably mindful of the increasing use of mobile apps around you. But it's still unlikely you're really cognizant of just how disruptive they will actually be over the next decade. Everything in business (and lots of other endeavors) runs on marketing. *Over the next 10 years, mobile apps will disrupt marketing more than newspapers, radio, direct mail, television, and the Internet did combined.* (And because you're in Leveraged Sales, you'd better read that last sentence again.)

Every process we perform in our business ultimately ends up being done on a smartphone:

- Prospecting
- Ordering
- Enrolling
- Marketing
- Communicating
- Training

We could delve into this deeper, but that's not really the point here. The real point is that our complete and utter devotion to smartphone mobile apps will impact every aspect of the business. Yes we have an alarming number of companies in our space that don't even have mobile-first websites. Or don't provide viable replicated websites for their distributors.

The companies in Leveraged Sales seem to be 10 years behind the curve here. And in the tech space, 10 years is like 100. (So for you company owners and execs reading this, you need to make this a top priority. And heed my advice about becoming a tech company first.)

BUILDING VOLUME WITH SOCIAL MEDIA

Now for you distributors, let's go back to something you have a lot more control over your social media accounts and how you can use them to develop your business…

Here's what I think may be the most relevant issue in our discussion: There is no longer an argument about doing the business "face-to-face" versus using technology like social media. Social media *is* face-to-face today. Seriously. That's just how people interact.

These days I find out when my nieces or nephews are getting married, having a baby, or going into the hospital from

Facebook. It wouldn't even enter their minds to actually call family members and give the news like that. And if you called them to express your hurt feelings because they didn't tell you, they'd respond accusingly, "Don't you follow me on Facebook?!"

The fact is, social media is an integral part of all of our lives and will continue to be so. And every business in the world, including ours, has to use it to varying degrees. But perhaps here is the most compelling thing to consider...

> *Employing social media in our profession is extremely efficient, effective, and enjoyable.*

Again, I will stipulate, it's important to not get sidetracked into the intricacies of the different platforms, because the platforms are in a state of constant flux. But the functionality and practices I'm about to describe will continue to be enduring and effective.

Allow me to submit a mix of some of the functions and practices that I see working right now, with a stunning degree of success...

Compelling Profiles

The point I'm about to make here may sound elementary, but it's vital. Make sure your profiles are set up to actually attract, not repel people. The clever pic of you quaffing a 64-ounce schooner of malt lager was cute in your college days. It's probably not doing you a lot of good now that you're a distributor for a wellness company. Find an inviting pic congruent with the type of image you want to portray.

It should go without saying (but won't) that if you're making snarky, insulting posts trolling people, you're going to lose a lot of candidates. Your online profiles are your organic résumé. If your bio starts with "If you support [name of political figure], please unfriend me right now," you're not going to win a lot of popularity contests.

Now, if you feel that you were placed on this earth to point out the failings of other people, and a supernatural entity anointed you to explain to others how stupid their political opinions are, by all means follow your passion. But please quit Leveraged Sales and become a cable network TV host.

Low-Key Independent Distributor Advertising

This is a simple practice that is picking up more and more steam. Some people are doing this in bigger ways with less duplicability by learning the skillsets of buying and targeting Facebook or Instagram Story ads.

Others are doing this much more simply, and with better duplicability, by simply working with the people who have already liked or followed them. Sometimes they are as low-key as promoting the benefits of their products or opportunity in their bio. They're just putting it out there for the people who may be interested. Others step it up a little higher by creating regular promotional posts or even placing camera-ready ads provided by their company in their feeds.

Live Online Streaming Presentations

Huge growth is happening in this area, one I'm a strong proponent of. In this case, you are taking the live nature and energy of hotel events and replicating them in a live, online format. As mentioned earlier, a member of our billion-dollar retreat is doing one each month to close out the month strong. They create a "show special" and alert all of the team members beforehand as to what the offer is. Then afterward, each member gets back with the candidates they sent to the presentation. They're enjoying extraordinary success selling the show special and building new customers.

Other companies with weekly pay plans are doing a similar plan, but with weekly shows. One twist that can up the energy and results even more is streaming shows "on location" from a live event with an audience in the room. The online group and the in-person group feed off the energy generated by each other.

These are especially helpful in new markets where the local team isn't yet large enough to have their own meetings with a large crowd. Bringing everyone together from around the country—or even the world—online creates the same kind of social proof and high energy that a huge offline meeting of 1,000 people produces.

And these streaming events aren't just limited to the traditional "opportunity meeting" presentations. Some distributors are essentially doing personal, QVC-type variety shows, entertaining their candidates and customers with folksy stories, humor, and viewer interaction—all while weaving in product offers.

Prerecorded Streaming Presentations

These presentations are pretty much the same dynamic as the live-streaming ones. The difference is that they are prerecorded and hosted on the company site or a social media platform. Then distributors have the option of contacting people in person, by app, through social media, or on the phone—and sending candidates to a specified link. In other cases, these distributors are regularly posting the link with a catchy write-up on their social media feeds.

Online Sample Offers

This is an approach that's working great for developing new retail customers. (Who frequently become builders down the road.) It's done by posting ads in your social media feeds for a special trial offer for a sample. A number of companies are having astounding success with products such as keto coffee or energy drinks.

There are a few different scenarios working well:

- The candidate pays a nominal amount (in the $3 to $5 range), ostensibly to cover shipping and handling.
- The distributor eats the costs, and the candidate gets the trial product for free.
- Or in some models, the ad is for the sample, and only after a candidate responds with interest does the distributor decide whether to send the sample free or ask for a small amount.

Online Product Trial Offers

This strategy works in a parallel manner to the small-fee or free-trial program above. Team members make an offer through a mobile app or in their feeds manually, but this time they are offering a larger selection: an entire package of related products. This might be at a $20 or $25 price point. This package offers a larger product quantity, with the idea of demonstrating a product result that might take longer to see. (A two-week weight loss program, for example.)

Creating Free Information Funnels

This is a marketing technique that's been around forever—just updated to harness the medium of social media. The idea is simple: Offer some information of value for free, with the goal of positioning yourself as a knowledgeable resource or friendly neighborhood specialist with helpful information. Once someone gets the free information (Special Report, video, booklet, etc.), you now have a qualified candidate to follow up with offers for your product.

Creating Product Benefit-Centered Groups

Another process is producing dramatic and powerful results for those doing it well. Distributors start a Facebook, WhatsApp, or

WeChat group centered around a topic like wellness, fashion, athletic performance, and so on. They populate the page or thread with continually added content: Live broadcasts, videos, pictures, and usually scads of testimonials. Then they use the group as a follow-up resource by inviting candidates and customers into the group.

Creating Branded Reseller Social Media Accounts

There are a couple of companies absolutely killing it with this strategy right now. It's a unique approach, very focused on creating large numbers of retail customers.

In the case of one of the companies, their product line is leisure and workout clothing. The basic scenario involves each new team member creating a new Instagram account—one specific for selling their product line. (The distributor doesn't use their personal account, even if they have one.)

Probably half of the company's initiation training is about setting up these Instagram accounts. They work with their people to make sure the account has a memorable handle, a great pic, and a fun bio that explains what they do in a catchy way.

Then the team member will send invites from their personal Instagram page and their other social media accounts to this new business page. (They also identify other people to follow who have similar interests, knowing that a certain percentage will look at their page and follow back.) It's all about making posts (about 80 percent product-centered and the rest fun and lifestyle posts). They might do 4, 7, or even 10 posts a day. (And people don't unfollow them, because it's a topic they are interested in.) These posts are done with appropriate hashtags so they also generate many new followers.

But the big day is once a week when new products are announced or old products are restocked. The company sends an email to all the reps (as well as having an Instagram support page for the reps), where they post videos explaining the new outfits and include pix. The reps can then resend the pix and videos or create their own Instagram stories about these new items. This particular company is growing like a weed and doing about 50 percent of their volume on these weekly launch days.

* * *

These are just some of the fun examples of how people are successfully building volume with social media in our profession today. The possibilities are endless and they'll evolve as both social media and our profession does.

This is definitely one of the areas in which you should counsel with your sponsorship line and explore what the best practices are for your specific company and product line. I simply wanted to spark your imagination and spotlight some of the exhilarating new strategies that are possible now.

I expect this chapter will create considerable debate in the profession. There are still a great many people who believe that strategies like these cannot be readily duplicated. But at this point, I believe that's missing the mark.

Is it really any harder to train someone how to search a hashtag—to follow appropriate people and engage with them—than it is to teach them an invitation script to use when calling someone? Yes, your new member orientation training will need to change. But I would argue that *all* your training needs to change. You have to reflect the reality of what's going on in the world today.

The other thing to consider here is that most of the people under 30—who are a huge active part of our business right now—already have the ability to work social media with mastery. They've been raised on smartphones and have never lived at a time without the Internet. They just need some simple guidance on how to brand their profiles and make the connection to what they're offering in a friendly and inviting way.

Next up, we're going to have an intense discussion about building profound depth and sustainable duplication...

CHAPTER 10

Creating Sustainable Duplication and Profound Depth

Newton's First Law of Motion

A body continues in its state of rest, or of uniform motion in a straight line, except insofar as it is compelled by external impressed forces to change that state.

Newton's Second Law of Motion

The rate of change of momentum is proportional to the impressed force and takes place in the direction of the straight line in which the force acts.

Newton's Third Law of Motion

It is an immutable dynamic of physics that the harder you close someone at your Direct Selling presentation, the less they will duplicate.

Okay, I lied. The third law is mine. And while I'm being cheeky here, I actually believe my law is as immutable as Newton's are. Here's why...

There is a variable that comes into play with Gage's Law, which isn't present in Newton's Laws: humans.

Unfortunately, if you want to build a large, successful team in Direct Selling, you're going to have to do it with humans. And humans are irrational, logical, methodical, impulsive, thoughtful, mindless, hurtful, loving, petty, generous, lazy, and ambitious.

And once you understand all that, humans are remarkably pre-dictable in certain scenarios...

Like when joining a Direct Selling business. Let's suppose you're making a presentation to a human. What you're offering doesn't seem all that desirable to them. You can sense that. But you're not worried...

Because you walked on frickin' fire with Tony Robbins and studied NLP. You've foreseen every objection possible and have a snappy clapback for them all. You pride yourself on the fact that you could sell solar panels to the ExxonMobil refinery, and you know every closing technique there is.

> **Your candidate:** "I'd like to talk this over with my wife and think about it some more."
>
> **You:** "Who wears the pants in your family? Aren't you the kind of person capable of making a decision?"
>
> **Your candidate:** "I like my job as a schoolteacher."
>
> **You:** "Do you realize how stupid it is to go to college and waste all that money on a degree? Don't you realize you're just a slave to your boss? You could be driving a Tesla instead of that beat-up Toyota you have."
>
> **Your candidate:** "You know, I kind of feel like you're a jerk."
>
> **You:** "I understand how you feel. I used to feel the same way. But here's what I found..."

Stop it. Just stop it.

Here's the thing people lose sight of. Sometimes you can sell some-one so hard, they will simply buy a distributor kit and a $400 activation order just to get away from you.

The harder you close someone, the less they will duplicate.

Why? Because duplication is created by people replicating the behavior you practiced with them. And if they feel uncomfortable doing that behavior, if it conflicts with the kind of person they are or want to be—they won't do it.

The reason some people build huge organizations and receive passive residual income for decades—while others have to furiously run on their hamster wheels to rebuild lines every few months—is because the first group understands duplication. They know the difference between *building* lines versus *driving* lines.

BUILDING LINES VERSUS DRIVING LINES

I told you that you build lines by people and process. Your growth is based on duplicable actions and creates yet more ongoing growth. People who drive lines do it with hype, and they must always keep it up relentlessly or their dropouts are greater than their new enrollments each month.

Building Blocks

When you build a line, you lay a foundation and consistently build on that foundation, creating a structure that will withstand challenges.

You construct a line with the building blocks we've discussed so far: adhering to the formula, knowing and following the system, and using third-party tools. All decisions are made with respect to how they will be able to be duplicated 10, 50, or 100 levels deep.

Contrast That with Driving a Line

You see this a lot from the dinosaurs and zombies I mentioned in Chapter 2. They're constantly flitting from program to program, looking for their next sweetheart deal.

"Heavy-Hitter Henry" discovers many of his distributors are dropping out and his check is constantly dwindling. (And the guaranteed income he received in his under-the-table deal is about to expire.) He knows it's time to move on to the next hot deal.

Henry starts a whispering campaign that he's available. And there's always another gullible company owner who thinks if he brings Henry aboard, Henry will roll over all of his team and instantly put the company on the map. Negotiations take place, a deal is struck, and secret payments are arranged.

Henry starts posting on social media announcing that he's "conducting research" on what the best opportunity might be. He invites everyone to present why he should consider their company. Of course, Henry isn't really looking at anything they send; he's already got his next deal negotiated. He's just accumulating contacts for his sucker list. Next he announces that after personally researching 139 possible opportunities, he's run an infallible analytical algorithm to determine the best one! Now the hype begins...

> *The fastest-growing company in the industry! Growing 1,346 percent a month! On track to be the next billion-dollar company...Find out why the Heavy Hitters are switching to ABC Company! CATCH THE WAVE!!! Call your downline before they call you!*

The live-streaming presentations commence with a steady diet of breathless sensationalism promising spillover and the chance to join "the fastest-growing company in history!" Sign-ups pour in.

There are no real relationships developed, no building blocks in place, and no company or product loyalty. Ninety percent of the new people will never even place a second product order. (Provided they even placed a first one.) Sponsoring plateaus, then begins to go south, and then Henry starts the process all over again.

I could name you at least five people—who for some unfathomable reason are considered leaders or top producers in our business—who do this three to five times a year.

How do these people maintain credibility and keep getting away with this 💩? Because they are dealing with humans. And humans sometimes let greed override rational thought, logic, and reality.

Even honest, well-meaning people sometimes resort to driving lines, though they're usually not aware of this...

They don't understand duplication and are frustrated with their people's inability to grow. So they start sponsoring yet more personal enrollees, stacking them under other people in the hope of forcing rank advancements, thinking this will motivate these people into better action. They do frenzied campaigns to drive volume at the end of a pay period, trying to qualify for a higher rank themselves. This might include pleas for their team members to stock up with extra orders to seal the rank advancement. That's driving with hype, not building with people and process.

Others Drive Lines by Becoming a Superhero

They make all the presentations, set up all the meetings, and do all of the trainings. They'll give away candidates and customers to people below them, hoping it will fire them up. They're the ultimate grinders, having to do everything for their team. If they ever slow down, sales and recruiting start to fall off. They're superheroes, but they will never appear in a Marvel flick and don't even get to wear the cape and tights. Ultimately, they end up frustrated with all of the codependent people in their group and drop out.

The Celebrity Lead Magnet

This is another scenario you need to watch out for. I've lost count how many times I have seen this play out in the past 20 years. A company hires a famous spokesperson, or the spokesperson joins as a distributor, or this famous person starts up their own company.

All the distributors are gaga over the halo effect this celebrity will have on recruiting. Usually this leads to major media campaigns inciting people to lock in a spot early—because of the steady stream of new people who will be joining the company, based on the association of this celebrity. In the worst cases, this gets promoted with television commercials and lead-generation co-ops are created. Thousands of leads pour in. But what happens at the end of the day?

The celebrity doesn't have a clue about how the business is actually built and usually doesn't even attempt to do the necessary work. In fact, the spokesperson has most likely been duped into believing that others will work the leads brought in by his or her name, and that a nice residual income will be the result.

This doesn't follow the formula for creating wealth in the business and is antithetical to the process of duplication. *The last time this worked successfully in the business is never.*

Driving lines like the examples above have nothing to do with building a long-term, successful business. You can create fast money for a short period of time, but nothing permanent. Stick to the building blocks and recognize that the most important strategy you'll employ is developing people.

SECURING A LINE

Back in the day, people would say that you don't leave a line until it's at least five levels deep or until the line reached a certain rank. In fact, you should never completely leave a line. Your role will change, however.

When you first enroll someone, you're intrinsically involved in the day-to-day building of the line, providing their fast-start training, helping with initial presentations, and teaching them the fundamentals. From there you evolve into the counseling stage.

Now, even though you are out of the day-to-day building, you play a much more important role—advising the leader of the line on a monthly basis. If you're doing your job right, this is the stage when growth should really start to take off in that line.

Ultimately, the head of the line should evolve into a top-level pin rank themselves. At this point, counseling may or may not be necessary any longer. You then evolve into more of a motivating presence for the line. You're the living example of someone who has made it, so your story and who you are inspire people in the organization. You will probably be the guest speaker once or twice each year at the larger meetings in their area.

You should always be supporting the line in one of these capacities. You will move from training to counseling when the person you're working with has the fundamentals down, and from counseling to a motivating presence after they secure the line.

By secure I mean that, even if you stop working with the line, it will continue to grow and provide passive income to you. A secure line doesn't require your day-to-day activity in it. Leaders have developed, more leaders are developing, events are happening, customers are being acquired, and business builders are being recruited. This happens only when you have enough core leaders in that line.

The reason that many people fail in Leveraged Sales is because they fail to identify and develop their leaders.

They spend too much time on metrics, like the number of people in their group or what their volume is, and don't spend adequate time facilitating the development of their leaders. They work only their pay levels or sometimes just with their personal enrollees.

To succeed at the high levels of Leveraged Sales, you must identify and work with your leaders, regardless of what level they are on. In fact, a lot of the time when you are building depth, you will be working way below your pay range. This is the only true method to secure lines.

Working in depth (with the people many levels deep in your organization) builds security. Working in width (sponsoring more personal enrollees) builds income. You need to do both to create a large passive income.

But you must *secure*, then *build*.

Only then can you move more into the inspirational or motivational capacity. And when you have lines secured, you then have the option to stop working and reap your residual income—or open new lines to expand your income.

Don't be deceived by high volumes or the number of distributors in a line. As we discussed earlier, high volumes and big enrollment numbers can be easily created by people driving lines. Make sure that your numbers are coming from the building-block fundamentals.

Lead by Example

Your number one obligation in the business is to become successful yourself. And then, of course, your second obligation is to help your team become successful. Most people get this mixed up.

They believe that you just make a bunch of people successful—and then you become successful. That theory sounds right, appears noble, and looks good on paper. But the reality is that you must become successful yourself first.

You can't show anyone how to build a team of 5,000 people if you have only 200 on yours. You can't demonstrate how to become a Diamond Director if you haven't yet attained that rank. If you really want to help your people, be the example by modeling the success behavior they need to know.

Now, on the other hand, don't create dependents. I have a strong and fast rule I live by. *Never do anything for a distributor they are capable of doing themselves.* Your job is to work yourself out of a job.

GETTING PEOPLE PAST THE BREAK-EVEN POINT

A big part of duplication is maintaining a high retention percentage. The lower your percentage of dropouts gets, the stronger your duplication will be. So the key is getting people past the break-even point as quickly as possible. This means they are earning enough money to cover their ongoing investment for the products they consume, their marketing materials, any self-development programs, and attendance at functions.

Here in the United States, that's probably around $5,000 a year in earnings for most people. In other parts of the world, the numbers will be different. Be mindful of what this income level is for your team. This is important because the people most likely to stay in and develop into leaders are people who have strong product affinity, practice daily self-development, and attend the major functions.

The disparity between team members who perform those activities and those who don't is massive. Once you can get people to this level, it doesn't cost any more out-of-pocket investment to work the business. Whatever they do from that point on will put them into profit. And because they are able to attend the functions and work on their personal growth, a huge breakthrough occurs...

They become leaders.

And developing new leaders may be the most important element in terms of your duplication. Because, for the most part, you won't sponsor as many leaders as the amount you develop from the team. And when you create a culture and process where you are developing leaders consistently, you'll have formidable, robust duplication. Once that is happening, your organization is going to start to branch out to other cities, states, or provinces, and maybe even other countries. Which is what we will explore next...

CHAPTER 11

Building a Business the Sun Never Sets On

The worst part of our business is you have to hop on planes and fly all over the country or the world.

The coolest part of our business is you get to hop on planes and fly all over the country or the world.

Both of the statements above are true.

One of the most frequent statements you'll hear from your new distributors is *"Hey, I have an incredible person in [city/state/ country]. Do we have anything going on there?"*

That's exciting to hear, as it could mean your group is about to have some strong growth in a new market. Unfortunately, this usually signifies something quite different.

This question often is generated because someone is looking for a distraction. Distractions mean people don't have to actually be building their business. And talking about or waiting to build teams somewhere else can serve as that distraction.

A team member will text you frequently, asking when Belgium is going to be opening, because they have an old college roommate there. Meanwhile, Germany, where they live and have 99 percent of their contacts, is already open. Instead of building their businesses locally, which they can actively do right now, they're fantasizing about a faraway city or country, because that gives them a chance to procrastinate.

Here's what you need to know and make sure each of your people knows...

Your local lines should be a large percentage of your income. You need to have a strong, sound, local organization that grows on a continuous basis. You should always begin with your local team and look at developing long distance lines in depth only after the local group is going.

Working in your local market is still the easiest, most cost-effective way to build. As you begin to develop depth, lines will start to expand into other states. By the time you get down seven or eight levels, it will not be unusual for you to be in 8 or 10 different states or provinces. But first you must develop a strong, local foundation.

LOOKING AT LONG DISTANCE LINES

Now, before we go further, let me clarify what I mean by a long distance line. If you can get off work at 5 p.m., drive to a market in time to start a meeting at 8, that is still a local line. I realize this requires serious effort and commitment, but this line can really still be handled in the same manner as your other local lines.

There are lots of good reasons to build long distance, but there are also some drawbacks if it's not done correctly. Let's get those drawbacks out of the way...

Long Distance Drawbacks

First, of course, long distance lines require a larger investment of both time and money than local ones do. Fly 1,500 miles to spend a weekend with a new line, and with everything added up you can easily spend $1,000.

Another drawback of working with long distance lines is that you cannot be there to look people in the eye when they experience challenges, or hug them when they celebrate victories. And sometimes your sitting across the table from one of their candidates at a two-on-one might be the very thing that gets that candidate in. But because newer services like ZOOM are increasing in quality all the time, creating a connection with people on the other end is becoming less and less of an issue. Still, it's not the same as your being in a city, working alongside your team member.

It's for these reasons that I encourage you to build a solid, local group first. This gives you the benefit of using the income you develop from your local lines to reinvest in your emerging long distance ones.

Long Distance Benefits

Okay, enough talk about the drawbacks. What about all the delicious reasons you should want to build long distance lines?

Having long distance lines is the best defense against the following scenarios:

- Overzealous government regulators
- Negative publicity
- Fluctuating economic cycles
- Loss of key leaders
- Natural (or even unnatural) disasters

Any one of the situations above could create complete financial ruin for you if your entire business is tied up with only one group or area.

Let's suppose you have a politically driven attorney general in your state who wants to run for governor. She's looking for some free publicity to build her name recognition. She decides the best way is to take on one of those evil, mean "pyramids," and she picks your company to go after. She's holding press conferences every day for two weeks as she attacks your company.

What do you think that kind of publicity would do to your income if it were on the evening news and cell phone alerts every night? The same thing can happen if the local newspaper does an investigative journalism series with the slant that Direct Selling is a rip-off, and your company is on the home page of their website all week.

If your whole group is local and the majority of it is less than one or two people, where will you be if they should leave for another opportunity?

Economic upturns and downturns can have a dramatic impact on your business. At the time I'm writing this, there are countries with an inflation rate of 100 percent—a month. The challenges of running a business in that environment are staggering. The closing of a large employer in a town can have a severe economic impact in that area. Sometimes that's good. Sometimes it's not.

Hurricanes. Earthquakes. Wildfires. Tsunamis. Tornadoes. Volcanoes. Mother Nature has more than a few surprises up her sleeve, and they're not always pleasant ones. Then throw in the manmade disrupters, such as epidemics, war, dictatorships, and Super Bowl parades, and you have a serious list of occurrences that can disrupt your business and income.

It's dangerous (and very foolish) to leave yourself at the mercy of circumstances you have no control over. The intelligent action is to protect yourself and diversify your income by sponsoring long distance. If your company just operates in one country, you want to have lines in all the different areas. And if your company is international, spreading your business between different continents is a very intelligent diversification strategy.

Here's something else to support this idea, something that might shock you...

> *The best-kept secret in Leveraged Sales is that your long distance lines are your strongest lines.*

Most people think it's just the opposite. They think that their local group is the strongest because they have the most people there. They see more people, more often, at functions. And there seems to always be people coming by their house, picking up marketing materials, borrowing products, or just looking for some friendly advice.

In actuality, your local line is often your most codependent line...

You'll notice that your people in a line 2,000 miles away don't call you when they need products; they don't poach an extra distributor kit when they run out; and they don't ask you to do the presentation for their hot new candidate. They maintain adequate inventory since no one is there to cover for them. Because they are far away from you, they become self-sufficient a lot quicker than your local lines do. Working long distance forces you to do what you should be doing anyway with your local lines—work yourself out of a job.

Other benefits...

If you're like me and enjoy traveling, you'll like having groups around the country (or the world) in scenic destinations. Long distance sponsoring is a wonderful way to finance your travel and get great tax breaks. It allows you to see some beautiful locales and develop new friends along the way. If your company has an aggressive international presence, you can develop a business where the sun never sets on it. You can go to bed at night, and there are people on the other side of the world making you money while you sleep. Think about that.

STARTING A NEW LINE

Okay, hopefully I've convinced you that building some long distance lines makes sense and you want to do that. Let's discuss some of the strategies that can ensure you accomplish this in the best way possible.

Follow the Market

The first thing I would recommend is to allow the market to direct you where to build, instead of trying to tell the market what you want. The latter option doesn't have a lot of successful practitioners.

Suppose your company announces that they are opening Japan. Well, that sounds romantic to you. You've always wanted to visit the Land of the Rising Sun and you love shrimp tempura. That by itself is not enough to justify building a line there. International flights are quite expensive, and you have no foundation to build upon, nor logical place to start.

Countless times in my career I have seen people become enamored with a foreign market and invest large sums of money to develop it from scratch. They rent an apartment for three months, pay for meeting space, run advertising, and hire translators. (I've even seen people pack up and move to a new country without knowing the language or anyone there.) In all the times I've seen this happen, never once has it actually worked.

Just because you love Italy or the idea of having a group in Australia, these aren't realistic reasons to build in those places. You want to let the demand rise organically within your team.

So when the company announces that they are opening Japan, the first thing to do is start polling your team. Is anyone from there, used to live there, went to university there, has any friends or relatives there? Make sure that there are actually enough contacts and potential in the new area to make launching the market viable. If there's not, pass it by and wait for another market with potential.

Don't succumb to pressure from your company to open in markets that don't make sense for you. I've seen situations where the company opens a particular market and pressures all of their top leaders to build there, whether they have connections or not. They are unknowingly being shortsighted. Not all executive teams actually understand how operations work in the field. As a leader, you need to protect yourself and your team from well-meaning but ignorant requests. (Even if they sometimes come from the company.)

When You Have Contacts in a New Market

Let's say a market is opening and it looks like you have some viable contacts there. (Or it's simply a case of having another city in a market you've already opened and you want to enroll someone there.) Here's the process I recommend.

Let your new candidate(s) know that this will be a long distance market for you, and if they want your support, they'll need to commit to being self-motivated, coachable, and able to follow directions. Advise them that you will be working with them online and by phone initially—with the goal of developing a core team before you travel there. Make the enrollment only if they agree to those terms.

If you're following my advice in this book, then you have some form of "fast start" or orientation for new members. (And if you don't have this, you'll need to use this book and assign them to go through Chapters 1 and 4.) Have them check in with you as soon as they complete this. Verify that they've placed their activation order, procured the marketing materials, and completed their candidate list.

Then help them launch their Major Blast, exactly as outlined. You can use ZOOM or FaceTime for their two-on-ones and first meetings and connect them with any online presentations your company is doing.

Of course, they'll want to know how soon you will visit their city and conduct an opportunity meeting or training for them. You're waiting to see at least 10 to 15 distributors, each doing their own Major Blast. Once that happens, it's time to schedule a visit. There should be enough critical mass to be worth the investment.

When you do go, give them benchmarks for when you return. Provide them with a stretch goal of a certain amount of attendance for their regular meetings, a certain number of builders, or some rank advancements. Agree to return when they reach that benchmark.

Traveling for Leverage

Your development to becoming a leader takes a big jump once you start to travel, support, and grow your long distance lines. Many people fight this, because they are starting to see some extra cash flow and want to use the money to juice up their lifestyle. But a smarter strategy is to reinvest that money into developing long distance lines. You'll jack up your income and create better financial security at the same time.

> *Be the number-one investor in your dream. If you don't invest in you, why would anyone else?*

A serious builder should be traveling one or two days a month. A mid-level rank should be out three or four days a month. And an elite pin rank with international lines may be traveling as much as 7 to 10 days a month. Those are my general guidelines, so please counsel with your sponsorship line on this. But make sure that every month you are investing in some long distance lines.

When you reach the point where you have a large team, one of the most important actions you will take to foster growth is choosing where to travel. Each month you'll check your back office, looking for sparks of emerging activity. Then you want to schedule trips to pour gasoline on those sparks and turn them into raging fires.

When you're new in the business, just traveling one or two days a month might be a challenge, because you've still got a regular job. You'll have to work around your days off and maybe use some personal and vacation days. But if you want to ultimately replace that job, you need to make a sacrifice at some point. As long as you follow the process I'm outlining here, your travel to long distance lines will be an investment—not an expense.

Let's look at one more strategy—a counterintuitive one that can have a rewarding return on investment for you...

Attracting Emerging Leaders

> *Sometimes the best approach to grow a team of leaders in another area isn't going to them—but getting them to come to you.*

You wouldn't do this with a new team. But if an area is developing, and some leaders are emerging, you might invite those leaders to make a field trip to your town for a few days. (And possibly offer to pay some of their expenses to help reduce the cost.) This can be a powerful tool if you have large successful events in your area. (Even better if you live near the corporate home office or manufacturing facilities.)

By attending these events in person, your new people get to see the exact outcome they are trying to create back in their own area. They witness some of the planning, setup, and execution of a large event. (Maybe even sit in on a special training session or simply have lunch with some of your local leaders.) The electric energy of the main event is sure to inspire these visitors and do the most important thing: build belief. So they will return home jacked up, with their hair on fire.

Next up, we're going to have a little fun—and study exactly what you should *not* do...

CHAPTER 12

Leadership Landmines That Kill Growth

We've spent 11 chapters looking at many strategies and techniques you can practice to grow your team and produce better duplication. Now is a good time to look at some of the actions and behaviors you should avoid. These are the "landmines" that actually inhibit or completely stop your growth.

When I conducted my Mega MLM Boot Camps, I created a workbook for that titled *The Direct Selling Hall of Shame*. The people "inducted" into this Hall were the ones who practiced behavior that would constrain leadership, kill duplication, and prevent achieving exponential growth.

To have some fun, I created personality profiles for each area of bad behavior. (I can assure you that there are thousands of people walking this earth whom these profiles are based on!) I've changed the names to protect the guilty. So without further ado, allow me to introduce them to you, in the hope you never appear on this list…

THE MARTYR

The Disease: The Martyr wants success for everyone so badly, he or she spends countless hours trying to drag people across the finish line. Most of the Martyr's time is spent trying to change people who don't want to change and save people who don't want to be saved. Martyrs operate on people's potential but ignore their actions.

How to Know If You're Infected: Ninety percent of your time is spent with your "problem children." You're so busy with them that you leave potentially great people to fend for themselves. Your best leaders are afraid to ask you for help, because you always seem so overwhelmed. In fact, you're so busy counseling, begging, and trying to motivate your problem kids, your own business suffers. You have difficulty keeping yourself motivated. Your group and your bonus check plateau and then start creeping backward.

The Cure: Spend 90 percent of your time with your real builders and do that first. Don't take talented people for granted and force them to work without your help. Partner with them, and only when their needs are met do you attempt to save the whiners, lost lambs, and charity cases. To help anyone reach success in the business—you must first become successful yourself.

THE TACTICIAN

The Disease: The Tactician believes that success in Direct Selling comes from knowing and teaching a method, strategy, or tactic for every conceivable situation.

Examples: "This is how you approach your girlfriend's boss. This is how you should approach someone in the subway. This is the script you use when someone asks if all of the ingredients are organic." The reality is that no one can effectively anticipate every possible scenario. And if someone could, no one would be able to duplicate them anyway.

How to Know If You're Infected: You're the ultimate grinder, getting hundreds of frantic calls, texts, and emails daily. You publish thick manuals of possible scripts and action steps, or spend hours every week training people to memorize scripts. You have a very high churn percentage in your group. The few people who stay out of loyalty or misplaced confidence (often accountants and engineers) replicate the process and become career grinders as well.

The Cure: You must resist the urge to develop a tactic and training for every conceivable situation and instead develop culture in the critical areas. You must create an environment where proactive people can learn to think for themselves. If you paint the right picture of the desired outcomes, people will figure out more than you might think.

THE MESSIAH

The Disease: The Messiah is the ultimate control freak. He or she believes that growth and motivation are created by developing a cult of personality. And since no one can measure up to the Messiah's standard of perfection, they must make all presentations, conduct all trainings, and be the all-knowing sage who solves all problems.

How to Know If You're Infected: Everyone in your group has your phone or email and turns to you first to solve all issues. This leads to overload, and people complain because you take forever to return messages.

You will experience rapid growth through four or five levels initially, where you can personally touch everybody with your magnetic personality. You do runs where you can drive large volume to reach a rank advancement, but you seldom requalify at that rank. If you're tech savvy, you might have more long distance groups, but you still handle every important presentation or training yourself, using the Internet, conference calls, video conferencing, or other tools.

The Cure: To get out of this mess, you must become the messenger, not the message. It's critical that you utilize third-party tools. You must delegate training functions and let your people conduct presentations—even when they can't do them perfect like you. You must limit access to you and your contact information to only personal enrollees and higher pin ranks. Make all issues work their way up through the sponsorship line and advance a level only when the person below cannot handle the issue. Instead of enjoying the satisfaction of solving problems for people, you must direct them where and how to solve their problems themselves.

THE SOCIAL (MEDIA) BUTTERFLY

The Disease: The Social Media Butterfly has been in 217 different deals in the past five years and assaulted their warm market so often and so obnoxiously, they're afraid to contact them again. Or they bought a $27 eBook titled *How to Become a Millionaire from Home While Watching the* SpongeBob SquarePants *Show*.

How to Know If You're Infected: You refuse to work your business in the outside world or talk with anyone you personally know. You prospect only strangers on social media or on spam lists you buy. You frequently appear on the top enrollers list, but you don't make any, you know, actual money.

The Cure: First, if you bought a course that teaches to approach only strangers, throw it away. You will never succeed until you become willing to talk with people you know and care about. And the best way to do this is with complete honesty and authenticity. If you really do relate to the example above, simply put the situation in the open. Say something like, "I know I've called you 217 times and thought I had the magic pill, and you have every right to hang up on me if you want to. But I have learned from my mistakes, and this time I honestly believe I have found something special. If you would be willing, just one more time..."

THE MAD GENIUS

The Disease: The Mad Genius believes that he or she has discovered a better way to do the business, one that the sponsorship line was too dim-witted to discover.

How to Know If You're Infected: Working the warm market is too boring and beneath you. Instead of following the system, you're always going for the big score. You want a short cut to the big bucks by sponsoring Meryl Streep, selling laundry soap to the Marriott hotel chain, or sponsoring the British Royal Air Force.

You spend months trying to become an approved government vendor, going through the purchasing process of large corporations, or chasing down the guy who mows the lawn for the lady who cuts the hair of the man that went to school with Lady Gaga. Leveraged Sales is not congruent with this business model, and the time you spend chasing the big deals kills any possibility of true duplication. You're probably frustrated and ready to drop out, because you haven't gotten any serious duplication for all of your efforts.

The Cure: Repeat this mantra 10 times each morning:

> "The big deal is the small deal... and the small deal is really the big deal."

THE FOLLOWER

The Disease: The Follower likes to stay behind the scenes and let someone in the sponsorship line be the face of their organization. They believe by lying low they will be easier to duplicate, or they have low self-esteem and don't believe they deserve to be on the stage. Unfortunately, this behavior is duplicated by the members of their team, who also decide to lie low and follow.

How to Know If You're Infected: When company leaders come to town, they can't remember your name. You shy away from doing presentations and don't want to be on the platform during training events. You're a good soldier who always attends all events and takes 17 pages of notes. You're in awe of bold people and like to be in their orbit.

The Cure: Show the spark and excitement that causes people to want to follow you. This doesn't mean create a new system but inspire people to follow your lead in the system. The person with the clicker makes the most money, so fight for your chance to be on the platform. Have a rock star photo and testimonial. Make your group proud to be on your team. Spend at least 30 minutes daily in self-development time to help resolve your worthiness and confidence issues.

THE MOTH

The Disease: Like that nocturnal insect attracted to any bright light, the Moth is elbowing their way into every opportunity for exposure. They want the spotlight so bad they'll walk over anyone and everyone, even their own people, to bask in the glow.

How to Know If You're Infected: You're always begging to be on the platform, angling for more exposure in the online presentations, and wanting to be featured in every tool the company or team develops. You've forgotten that the actual objective here is building a sustainable business, not getting more stage time.

The Cure: Humility. Recognize that everything is not all about you. And even in cases where your work and achievements make you deserving of more exposure, sometimes the best course of action is to allow other developing leaders to be featured.

THE OSTRICH

The Disease: The Ostrich's highest value is avoiding confrontation. She wants to be liked, so she tells people only what she thinks they want to hear. When problems arise in the group, the Ostrich ignores them and hopes they go away. When her team members come to the Ostrich with ideas that will take them off course, she doesn't want to hurt their feelings, so she panders to them.

How to Know If You're Infected: Your sponsorship line or the company is calling you with problems that your group took to them. Small issues snowball into divisive conflicts. Your team does not feel protected by you. You have lots of people off-system who are struggling, and you keep hoping someone up the sponsorship line will swoop down and save them.

The Cure: Confront problems head on immediately. Deal with problem people with kindness, tact and grace—but exercise "tough love" when they exhibit behaviors that will hurt their own business or others. Care for your people enough to tell them the truth, especially when they are in danger of getting off-track.

THE PRINCE(ESS) OF DARKNESS

The Disease: This person knows why every new initiative will fail and their career becomes a self-fulfilling prophecy. Instead of a healthy skepticism, they bring toxic cynicism to the party.

How to Know If You're Infected: You're a professional victim who attracts drama and trauma continuously. If there are isolated cases of missed commissions, late shipments, or back office glitches—you trumpet them as an epidemic and cite as "proof" the business can't work. This flies in the face of the fact that other people are succeeding under the same circumstances. (Cynics always find a way to prove their limiting beliefs.)

You become a one-person distraction factory. Your need to commiserate with other victims causes you to send negativity down your team, sabotaging any chance at growth. You have meager bonus checks and growth comes in fits and starts with no duplication. Which just proves what you've believed all along.

The Cure: The only cure for this disease is relentless daily self-development. This involves a long-term process of reprogramming your subconscious mind to convert limiting beliefs into empowering ones. To earn more, you must become more.

THE PARTY ANIMAL

The Disease: The Party Animal is an alcoholic and hasn't accepted the truth. They believe they're just being social and communing with their team, but in actuality, they're creating serious impediments to not only their progress but their team's as well.

How to Know If You're Infected: Hitting the bar after every event. Losing respect among your team members because you acted foolishly or made inappropriate advances or comments after too much to drink.

The Cure: Alcoholics Anonymous. And for companies (especially health and wellness ones): Stop providing open bars on every cruise or leadership retreat.

THE SALES PRO

The Disease: The Sales Pro is usually a grizzled veteran of old school high-pressure sales and closing techniques. They don't understand the difference between pitching a tourist to buy a timeshare they don't need versus creating duplication through leverage.

How to Know If You're Infected: You sponsor large numbers of people, but almost none of them duplicate—except other sales types. You think you're too talented to use third-party tools. You would much rather conduct one-on-ones to make sure you get the close. You have canned scripts for every possible objection and have constructed a Jeffrey Gitomer shrine in your bedroom.

You appear on the top enrollers list at first, but become so frustrated with your lack of duplication that you consider quitting or "putting the business on the back burner for a little while." Your initial bonus checks looked great because of the volume from new enrollments, but your residual income wouldn't feed a church mouse.

The Cure: The secret here is to make sure your sales skills don't get used against you. Closing techniques *work*, but they don't *duplicate*. The mantra for rehabilitating Sales Pros is:

"If your lips are moving, you'd better be pointing to a tool."

THE BFF

The Disease: The BFF wants to be Best Friends Forever with everyone they sponsor. Unfortunately, familiarity breeds contempt.

How to Know If You're Infected: Your team is so familiar with every little detail and problem in your life that they have no respect for you. As a result, they can't properly edify you, limiting your ability to help them grow. Every opportunity meeting has the same usual suspects attending. What should be business functions become primarily social ones.

The Cure: Keep your professionalism with your team at all times. If you must regale someone with the details of your recent bunion surgery, call your sponsor. A little mystery goes a long way.

THE BLIND, HUNGRY DOG IN A BUTCHER SHOP

The Disease: The BHDIABS is so excited and they want success so badly, they are always looking for a shortcut to grow faster. They have an attention deficit personality, get bored easily, and have difficulty focusing.

How to Know If You're Infected: You fall prey to the "flavor of the week" syndrome. You're always investigating what other lines are doing and trying to infiltrate calls and meetings from other companies to learn their "secret." You want to buy leads, build online only, skip meetings, or take a commercial spot during the Oscars. You have fits of quick growth, followed by sharp volume dips when the hot new recruiting burst ends. Eventually, your team becomes disillusioned with lack of focus and consistency and they lose faith in you.

The Cure: Follow the formula for creating wealth in our profession: *Empower a large group of people to perform a few simple actions on an ongoing basis.* System, system, system.

THE RENEGADE

The Disease: Renegades always want to prove that they are so special that they don't need the system. Or that they are so smart they can think of a better system. Often they wrongly believe those techniques that worked in the corporate world or to sell used cars will work in Leveraged Sales. Even though they're only earning $800 a month, they're convinced they have discovered something that the people earning $40,000 a month haven't figured out.

How to Know If You're Infected: You don't have time to participate on team webcasts and events. You're not plugged into the system, so your sponsorship line can't really help you. You hold their own team calls and functions, or you're always in the hallway during group events. You create fast rank advancement for yourself at first, causing other lines to wonder if they are missing out on something. But ultimately you have a hard time staying qualified at rank and don't have many people on your team breaking ranks either.

The Cure: There is no known cure for this disease. But researchers have seen promising results with humility and a willingness to be coached.

THE HOMETOWN PROPHET

The Disease: Hometown Prophet Syndrome occurs when someone stays exclusively in their hometown too long, and the business stagnates.

How to Know If You're Infected: Because the people in your local group recognize that they are 90 percent of your group and your income—they start to lose respect for you. Then they can't edify you properly, so you can no longer create excitement and inspire the team to action. The opportunity meetings become monotonous and team members outnumber guests 25 to 1. Because there are no fresh success stories, eventually your group begins to decline.

The Cure: Protect your financial security and diversify your business by building long distance. Start by developing a beachhead locally, then expand your range as you see sparks of leadership developing in other areas.

Check your back office each month looking for pockets of growth. When you see a potential leader, go down in the group and taproot the excitement and activity back up the line. Never let one person's line account for more than 60 percent of your volume.

THE SHREWD INVESTOR

The Disease: The Shrewd Investor thinks there is a communist conspiracy to get all their money by forcing them to buy marketing tools and tickets to functions. They believe they can outsmart the Commies and save their way to becoming a millionaire.

How to Know If You're Infected: You refuse to attend functions because you think you have a better use for the money they require. If you do buy recruiting tools, you're saving them for a better candidate. Or you knock off marketing materials and use cheap copies instead. This culture has duplicated through your team, and any growth you see is incremental. Then you see the slow growth and small bonus checks as more proof that you should be saving your money instead of investing in your business.

The Cure: Businesses grow in direct proportion to what is invested in them—mentally, time-wise, and financially. Meetings make money and create rank advancements. Attend all major functions and develop that culture in your team. Stop buying stories—your own and others'—and exercise the discipline and tough love to get people to events until they get over the line.

THE HELICOPTER SPONSOR

The Disease: The Helicopter Sponsor is always hovering over their enrollees, trying to protect them from any mistakes or adversity. They are well meaning, but they actually hurt their people by making them codependent. They solve problems for their people instead of teaching them how to figure things out.

How to Know If You're Infected: Your people call you constantly to ask you questions like where the meeting is, what time it starts, what's the CV of a product, or whether you have extra marketing materials they can borrow. When they have a problem with an order or payment, they contact you first. You have people still asking you to stream into their one-on-one presentation even though they joined the business in 2008. You get messages asking you why you haven't put anyone in their group this month. Your team members use your house as the satellite warehouse. You're the only person in your town who can conduct presentations or training. You're a grinder.

The Cure: Never do anything for a team member they are capable of doing themselves. When your people encounter a problem, instead of solving it for them—teach them the skills and give them the information they need to solve their own problems. Remember: Your job is to work yourself out of a job.

Teach people how to fish. If they demand the all-you-can-eat fish fry, direct them to another restaurant.

THE HOLLYWOOD DIRECTOR

The Disease: The Hollywood Director starts off strong and brings in some people quickly. Then they go into Spielberg mode, thinking their job is to just direct the action.

How to Know If You're Infected: You never have any candidates at presentations yourself, because you are too busy messaging your group to ask how many candidates they are going to have. The last time you personally sponsored someone was during the Bush Administration.

The Cure: Even at the highest pin levels, the best leadership and training you can provide is to model the behavior you want your people to emulate. That means staying active in the sponsoring process yourself.

THE CON MAN (WOMAN)

The Disease: The Con Man believes that the end justifies the means. They may compete with their team for recruits, frontload people, lie to their team, or manipulate them in ways that are not in the best interests of their business.

How to Know If You're Infected: You have high churn rates, low volume, and your team members don't trust you. Other lines may ostracize your group or bar them from functions.

The Cure: Nothing is more important in our profession than good character. Make and keep the following two promises to your group:

1. I will never knowingly lie to you.

2. I will never knowingly tell you anything that isn't in the best interest of your business.

* * *

Note: There are other case studies that were not explored here but could have been. They include the Liar, the Addict, and the Cheat. If you develop a reputation for getting stoned at events, sleeping with someone else's spouse, borrowing money without repaying it, breaking promises, or displaying other character defects, you will quickly lose all respect and credibility with your team.

If you have a substance abuse problem, get professional help. If your actions won't stand up in the light of day, don't do them. Even if it costs you initially, always do the right thing. Ultimately, you will prosper.

All right, now that you've seen many of the habits and behaviors that prevent you from becoming a leader—let's switch the perspective and look at how you build your personal leadership brand...

CHAPTER 13

Building Your Personal Leadership Brand

Note: This is the first of the five bonus chapters. If you're just starting out in the business, please skip this chapter, along with the next four (Chapters 14, 15, 16, and 17) for now, and jump to Chapter 18. Come back and look at these chapters two years from now when they will be much more relevant to you.

The entire concept of personal branding is kind of a recent development in the culture. In the past, personal branding wasn't even a recognized term, even though some individuals did create brands. Elvis, JFK, Marilyn Monroe, and many others most certainly cultivated certain images and became iconic individuals. But we didn't view the public's perception of these figures as branding at the time. We simply thought they were famous people and branding applied only to companies and certain products.

Today, personal branding is a phenomenon.

There are 13-year-olds chatting with each other about their brand on Instagram. Seriously. So this phenomenon does impact our profession. And has become part of the equation in terms of building a large, successful team, both for key company executives and field leaders.

(And this is another issue that some short-sighted companies or leaders might not like. They don't want their leaders developing a brand or following, because they fear that leader could leave in the future, causing their team to follow them. But this is fear-based thinking. And doesn't reflect the actual situation today.)

There are a few dynamics that cause this new reality. Let's explore them.

DYNAMICS OF PERSONAL BRANDING

One of those dynamics is the aforementioned social media. Presidents and popes, authors and evangelists, experts and authorities—they all seem to have social media accounts. So by transference, people have come to expect leaders in all spaces to be on social media. When they're not, their legitimacy almost seems suspect. (And yes, some leaders may undermine their legitimacy with their posts, but that's a topic for another day. For most leaders, social media advances their work.)

One of the other dynamics is that people feel more comfortable following someone who is branded in a certain way. The brand could be around a variety of possibilities: decisiveness, strength, compassion, empathy, and so on. The point being that leaders stand for something, and the people who choose to follow them know what that particular something is. (Not always consciously. More often, unconsciously.)

The final dynamic that's relevant here is what the branding of a leader does for the leader herself. Creating and maintaining a brand requires thoughtfulness. The process makes you do some serious critical thinking about what you will stand for, how you want to be perceived, and hopefully, what you are remembered for. This type of contemplation has the potential to dramatically impact and influence the culture your organization will develop.

Taken together, these dynamics all demonstrate the benefits and necessity of building a personal brand in today's environment. We'll explore that a little deeper, and of course we'll discuss how to best do that.

But there's a catch...

You don't get to "control" your brand. Other factors outside of your control dramatically impact it. More about this in a minute...

And then we need to deal with the issue of duplication: creating your personal brand in a way that doesn't hamper people's ability to replicate your results. That can get a little messy. So let's revisit some of my thoughts on branding from *Risky Is the New Safe* and update them into what you're facing in our space today.

THE REAL TRUTH ON BRANDING

A brand is really a meme-plex—a collection of related memes, aka mind viruses. And nothing spreads memes faster than the Internet. When Nike creates a YouTube sensation like "Write the Future..."; when millions of people tune in to see Tim Cook launch a new Apple product; whenever someone tweets or posts a review on a website, updates their Facebook status, or adds a pin about their new iPad—memes are flying and branding is taking place.

The goal is getting that process to happen about you, your team, and special events you are conducting. Obviously, this won't be on a worldwide scale like some of these examples above. But it's the same process on a smaller scale.

Navigating the minefield of branding and positioning has never been easy. Now the process is getting more complex. While you couldn't control your brand in the past, you could at least try. Social media has made that close to impossible now. However, the flip side is that you really know what your brand represents in the marketplace and when you need to fix something.

I told you the best products for Leveraged Sales are products that are unique, exclusive, and highly consumable. And you know what products are best for creating branding buzz? Products that are unique, exclusive, and highly consumable.

The company you represent has a brand. Your product line may have a separate one or be a part of the bigger brand. But in either event, your brand is not the logo or tagline.

Your brand is how the market perceives you.

And that is created by the experience your customers, candidates, and team members experience. The Internet allows people to share those experiences more readily, and that has impacted branding in a big way.

And, of course, social media has made branding more than interesting…

On the surface, your brand is how the market perceives you. On a deeper level, your brand is how the market perceives what you can do for them. But at the ultimate, ultimate level—and now we're in the rarified air of brands like Apple, Cirque du Soleil, Starbucks, and Nike—your brand is how you make the consumer feel about him- or herself.

That 350-pound guy you see taking the escalator? He would get winded in a chess match. But in his mind, he's an elite athlete because he's wearing a sweatshirt that says, "Just Do It!"

I'm an old guy who took about two years to figure out how to send an emoji. But I use a Mac. So when I walk in that Apple store, with all those skater kids, people with their dogs, and the rad guys at the Genius Bar—the environment makes me feel cool!

The same is true for the people you see in line for their half-decaf, double-mocha-froth, carmelata-frutata-frappuccinos at Starbucks; the ones browsing around in the Nike superstores; and those mesmerized by a performance of Cirque du Soleil. They are passionate advocates of the product they are buying—really, the product they are *experiencing*.

They believe in what they buy and want to share their experience with everyone they know. They move from customers to a marketing team more powerful than any amount of money can ever buy. This is the epitome of what Seth Godin describes in his brilliant book *Tribes*.

When your brand attracts a tribe, it can make you rich. And nothing inspires a tribe more than making people feel a certain way about themselves. Nike makes everyone feel like an elite jock; Starbucks admits you into the clubhouse; Apple lets you be one of the cool kids; and Cirque takes you to an enchanted place.

Before each of his concerts, singer Jimmy Buffett does a live "tailgate party" on Radio Margaritaville, talking about the venue, set list, any guest stars, and just generally being a raconteur. The show is probably as perfect a demonstration of how to use social media and technology to engage with a tribe you'll ever see. So here's some food for thought...

How can you create this shared identity and sense of community in your team?

How do you want your personal brand to make your team feel about themselves?

What if you streamed a tailgate party before your next convention?

POSITIONING YOURSELF AS A LEADER

Let's leave the macro and look at the micro. Think about when you've been on a plane, it hits some turbulence, the pilot comes on the PA, and—in a relaxed voice, maybe even with a yawn—gives a reassuring update. She projects that calm, almost-bored tone to keep the passengers from panicking.

Or when a couple is getting divorced and the kids become aware that their world is fracturing. They're frantic, desperate to know that Mommy and Daddy are still in control and everything is going to be all right. That's what you have to do as a team leader.

And that's why I believe having a personal brand is so important in the Leveraged Sales business.

Some of you may be thinking, "Well, I'm not really comfortable being out front, being on stage at the events, or being one of the faces of the leadership team."

Sorry, that dog don't hunt.

Not if you want to be a strong leader and give your team the most supportive infrastructure to develop and grow. Here's what you need to be considering…

> *Your people anxiously want (and need) you to be a leader. They need you on the stage. They want to take pride in your leadership and feel the satisfaction of ownership (and sense of belonging) that comes with being on your team.*

Please read that last paragraph again. And really process that information. Like the pilot of that distressed plane or parents in a divorce, you need to be the calming, stabilizing influence. And what your brand is, and how you are positioned, will greatly impact your effectiveness in doing this.

The one *huge* difference in Leveraged Sales versus any other business in the world is the need for duplication. So let's get something vital out of the way right now.

> *I am not suggesting you talk about any of this in your new member orientation. Don't make a peep about this to any beginning distributor. What we're discussing here is for leaders who are going to build a team of at least 10,000 people. This is a conversation you probably have with someone after they've been in at least two years.*

We need to stair-step people in their learning process.

Stage 1: How to get customers

Stage 2: How to enroll builders

Stage 3: How to run a home-based business

Stage 4: How to manage an organization

Stage 5: How to lead people

This issue of personal branding should be taught to your leaders only at Stage 5. And then when we do that, we have to navigate the delicate dance of positioning people as leaders—yet not disrupt the essential process of duplication we need to take place.

So, in that view, please don't think (or teach) that every leader needs to be an outside consultant, author books, conduct public seminars, or take actions of that nature. Some of us have outside ventures for various reasons. But there's no need for you to mimic that process to build your personal leadership brand.

One of the biggest issues I see in the profession is leaders who think success comes from building up their own image as a superhuman achiever. You may look great in a cape and tights, but you will create a lot of star-struck followers unable to replicate your results. You suck all of the oxygen from the room. So you don't need a million-dollar deal for an autobiography from Simon & Schuster or your own prime-time TV show.

Let's just position you as someone with credibility, authority, and expertise—whose team others will want to be a part of.

There are a few staple items that are extremely helpful in positioning you in the personal brand space you're looking for.

1. Photo Shoot

The camera in a smart phone today is the equivalent of a camera that used to cost $1,500. Yet I am continually shocked that when I ask a leader—someone who will be presenting at a major event—to send a recent pic, they can't. They don't have one. In 2019. Typically what they send me is blurry, has terrible lighting, looks 15 years old, or has them preening with plump Aunt Gertrude in her bikini at a water park.

By the time you're attaining a leadership position, you should invest in a photo shoot with a professional photographer. And also make sure you are capturing lots of video and pix on your award trips at those luxury resorts around the world. Ultimately, you want to have four types of photos:

1. A head shot
2. A three-quarter head and shoulders shot
3. A business "action" shot
4. Lifestyle photos and videos

These photos and videos can be used for event flyers, business cards, and websites. Often your company will design recruiting materials and want action and lifestyle clips from team members to showcase success. Make sure you have them in case you're asked.

2. Your Story

This is the background that provides context, gives social proof, and allows candidates to connect with you. Mine is that of a high school dropout who went from minimum wage dishwasher to multimillionaire. Andi Duli was an immigrant pizza delivery guy, Sarah Robbins was a schoolteacher, and Erick Gamio was a head-banging rocker.

Your story doesn't have to be a "used to be sleeping under a bridge" story. The story of someone who walked away from a prestigious, high-paying "status" job to work from home and spend more time with their family can be just as powerful. *Real and relatable is much better than hype and hoopla.* This story is what your team members tell their friends on the phone when they're inviting them to come and see you speak.

The whole point of the story is to let both candidates and team members find commonalities in their own experience, so they can "put themselves in the picture." The other objective your story accomplishes is making it easy for candidates to see what your team culture is really about. So they know if they want to be a part of this type of group.

3. Your Bio

This is the written, "official" encapsulation of your story. The one people will use on the flyers and websites promoting an event when you are appearing. Your bio need only be a few sentences. But it's shocking how many people in our space have never thought this out. This is where you mention that you're the #7 income earner in the world, built a team of more than 10,000, have team members in 21 different countries, or reached the rank of Diamond Presidential Super Blood Wolf Moon Supreme Commander.

Just the simple act of providing a pic, bio, and story for your team allows you to be dramatically more effective in supporting them. They use these tools to edify you, and then you are able to come down in the group and edify what they are doing. And by providing your team with these tools, you are modeling the behavior they will need to adopt as they progress into the leadership ranks.

These three simple tools—a bio, story, and photo—will play a big part in creating the positioning you're looking for. The cool thing about all this is you get to choose what you want to be about. Think about some of the different ways people in our business approach this:

Chris Brady and Orrin Woodward are best known for their leadership expertise because of their work and books on that topic.

Lily Rosales has mad skills in leadership, recruiting, and team building. But the personal branding she is best known for is her "cuchi-cuchi"—the love and empathy she demonstrates to people.

My brand is centered on my gifts at systems and duplication. People join my team because they're confident they will achieve duplication.

But perhaps the best personal branding in our space was Dexter Yager. A former beer truck driver, his brand was "Everyman." Every candidate got the feeling that if Dexter achieved success, they could, too.

As you think about your personal branding and positioning, focus on how and what you want to be remembered for one day. Then have fun with the exercise. But before we leave the subject, it's vital you understand the real objective here…

The goal isn't to make you an iconic leader who is worshiped and revered. The desired outcome is that your team knows who you are, what you are about, how you inspire them and make them feel.

The crucial result you're looking for is to become a leader who inspires others to leadership. Great leaders don't develop people's belief in the leader; they develop a belief in the follower.

> *Your true test is not how many followers you have—but how many leaders you develop.*

And that's what we will explore next…

CHAPTER 14

How You Become a Positive, Powerful Leader

BREAKING NEWS: Nobody wants to watch the movie about the billionaire who bought a lotto ticket and won another $40 million.

But the slumdog who becomes a millionaire—we'll buy a ticket for that every time…

So you earned a free bonus car. You're delirious with excitement and your mom is really proud of you. Truth is, the rest of us don't really care.

Because it's not really about your car. It's what your car can mean to the rest of your team. And the same is true for that luxury cruise you won, the big bonus checks you're cashing, and the $50,000 watch you're wearing.

Contrary to popular belief, nobody on your team is going to build better or bigger because you got a snazzy new Philippe Patek "timepiece." In fact, a lot of times, all the check-waving and frenzy are a turnoff and *uninspire* people.

Here's why…

No one wants to hear how rich, sexy, marvelous, and happy you are. Or at least they don't until *after* they've heard how poor, unattractive, mediocre, and miserable you used to be.

It seems everyone is trained to tell their "story" in Direct Selling. And they think their story is all the bling, bonuses, and big bucks they made. But that doesn't inspire people. Here's the most important thing you should know when you're sharing your story or a testimonial...

> *The only reason you tell your story is for the lesson or inspiration it holds for the audience. Anything else is just beating your chest.*

Your story is inspiring only if it teaches that you have faced some of the challenges, obstacles, and adversity the people who are listening to you are facing. The fact that you persevered inspires them to know that they, too, can persevere.

It shows you are qualified to teach them.

Like great authors or motivational speakers, we don't tell our story because people are interested in our story. We tell our story because of the impact it can have on the audience.

And when you understand this, you are on your way to becoming a visionary leader in our profession. Because then you realize that it is never about you. True leadership is always about the results for the people you lead.

A couple decades ago, I was asked to give my definition of leadership for a book on that subject. I defined it then as the ability to cause people to willingly take actions they wouldn't normally want to do. (For example, in a war, someone charges a machine gun nest to protect their unit. In our business, it may be as simple as someone buying their first suit or making their first speech in front of a group.)

That definition suited me for more than 20 years. But no longer. My thoughts have evolved, and here is how I would define leadership today:

> *Inspiring people to become the highest possible version of themselves—and building the environment that facilitates this process.*

To elaborate more, this defines *positive* leadership. (Because we know all leadership is not always constructive and encouraging.) I believe my new definition best defines how leadership should look in our space—and is the model you should aspire to.

You can see there are two very distinct parts of that equation above. The first part is inspiring people to want to take the action and do the work of becoming the highest possible version of themselves. That's difficult enough, even for world-class leaders.

But next you've got to go one step further and create a structure that allows your team to do that. (By the culture you set, the system you develop, the resources available for people to implement, etc.)

Stepping into the Rare Air of Leadership Greatness

Let's say you have reached the point where you have a large network, you're producing high volume, and people are looking to you for guidance. How do you become a superlative leader for your team? How do you create group action and a shared purpose, inspiring your team into action?

> *A big component of this is influence. If you really do want to inspire people to become more and create a safe space for them to do that, you must become a powerful influencer yourself.*

Let me share with you the tools and actions I have found to be the most successful for influencing a large team…

Build a Dream Bigger Than the Team

Too many people who want to be leaders are trying to push people when they should be pulling. To create buy-in, it's important that you articulate a bold, valiant, and compelling outcome that speaks to the aspirations of your people.

Everyone everywhere possesses an innate desire to become part of something bigger than themselves. Nothing else in our lives provides such a tremendous feeling of satisfaction and belonging as being intrinsically connected to a force, project, or movement for good.

Your team will get excited about the contests and promotions and chase after the free trips, bonus cars, and other rewards. But if you can pair that pursuit of profit with a plan for higher good—they'll certainly become yet more energized. Sometimes this is moving toward a positive result, such as building an orphanage. Other times it may be fighting a common foe that your product line addresses (Big Pharma, the insurance companies that are ripping off people, etc.).

Demonstrate Your Commitment

We all know people who talk a good talk, but it's all eyewash. Nothing will delight your team more than seeing evidence that you aren't practicing empty talk. Show that you have an unyielding, unwavering force toward the vision, and you're doing everything possible to get there yourself.

Maintain Laser Focus

You're dealing with people, so there is always going to be gossip, petty jealousies, and those who want to hijack the agenda for their own attention or ends. Kill distractions immediately.

As part of leading a sales team, you'll probably have to be forceful to hold people accountable and take action where necessary. (In particular, the next three items will be quite helpful in this regard.)

Practice Inclusion

Creating a benchmark activity to qualify for rewards can become a powerful inducement to produce desired behavior. These can be anything—minor perks, like preferred seating at events, to major opportunities, such as trips and retreats.

A powerful driver of behavior can be an inner circle that people want to be a part of. People want access to the leadership team, and they will be willing to work hard to gain this admittance. It's very important that there is no element of politics or favoritism. This must be a meritocracy, not a teacher's pet scenario.

Practice Exclusion When Appropriate

Create a healthy desire in people that motivates them to reach goals the next time. Leave them hungry to get into the next level. Let me give you a specific example of where this has worked exceptionally for me.

We would include a "Brilliance Banquet" at our major events, with invitation limited to only those who qualified at certain ranks. We would take them by stretch limo to a fabulous nightclub for dinner. They would meet in front of the hotel in tuxes and gowns, taking pictures with the limo. We encouraged the people who did not qualify to come down and watch, to "feel the burn" and make the commitment that they would qualify for the next event.

It's important to use discernment in how this is handled. You don't want it to feel like, "You're a loser; you didn't qualify." You want to create the vibe, "You've got to be with us next time!"

Place Expectations on People

You need to see people's greatness and potential even before they do themselves. Let them know you expect exceptional results from them. Many of them will borrow this belief you have in them until they are able to develop it for themselves. This is possibly the greatest gift you can bestow on the people who follow you.

Repeat Core Messages

Never lose sight of foundational principles. The message is never old to new people, and old people need to be kept on track.

202 Direct Selling Success

You're going to need to repeat training segments on core competencies like recruiting, meeting people, and inviting every time you do a major event. Every. Single. Time.

Forever.

The real work here is making sure to keep the message fresh and relevant, even though the primary information pretty much remains the same.

Create Intensity

Be bold, be passionate, and be intense. Foster a culture of action, urgency, and passion.

Provide Game Plans

Some people will know the path to follow to achieve what they want. Others will need more assistance. So outline a structured, attainable game plan to follow. Teach people how to create campaigns to advance their game plan. (Building to the next major event, for example.)

Offer Recognition and Rewards

Be generous with public praise for activities well done, projects completed, and rank advancements achieved. Utilize contests and other incentive programs where appropriate.

Recognize. Praise. Celebrate.

Use Group Dynamics and Social Proof

Most people today are afraid to speak up, stand out, or make an independent decision. Social proof can be a forceful resource to entice them to step out of their shell. People take actions more readily if they see others taking that action.

Simply using examples and case studies of strategies that other leaders in the team have employed successfully will provoke many more to take the leap. This is why testimonials are so effective in recruiting, sales, and marketing—and getting people to reach higher.

As a leader you must help people grow and prod them to increase the pace of that growth. Use people's insecurities against them in a positive way—a way that inspires them to transform those limitations into strengths. When you see "sibling rivalry" between teams, utilize that to stimulate them to do better.

Practice Two-Category Coaching

I'm sure you'll be shocked to learn that some people like to whine a lot. And others are always looking for distractions and excuses. These people are the ones that want to suck up all your time and energy.

Here's how you deal with this in an exquisite way to remain productive and provide the best support for your entire team.

Mentally divide your team into two categories: those you work with personally, and those you work with through group interaction. When you get someone who has true leadership potential, is coachable and willing to work—give them all the personal attention they need.

When you're being hounded by someone complaining about variables that can't be changed, wants to gossip about someone else, or just likes to hear themselves talk—direct them to a group resource.

Examples:

> **Them:** "Why did the company make the label on the energy bar red? The people in my area like the color blue a lot more…"

You: "Hey, why don't you come early to the training event on Saturday, and we can talk it over then?" (Don't worry—they won't show up anyway.)

Them: "I have a friend and they only eat plastic and gravel, because they believe it's morally wrong to kill plants. They refuse to buy our protein powder because it includes murdered rice. I think there's a huge market of gravel eaters that we're missing out on. I'm afraid to contact any more candidates until this important issue is resolved. Can we schedule an emergency meeting with the CEO, advisory board, marketing department, and me to get this handled?"

You: "That's an interesting question. Be sure and watch the online training on Tuesday, and I'll try to deal with the issue of marketing to different subsets of the market."

If someone has a legitimate concern, of course you should always address it. But you'll quickly learn which people are just looking for excuses to avoid doing any actual work. Direct them to the group interactions and limit your personal interactions and time with them.

Practice Accountability

One of the issues you'll encounter frequently when counseling with your people is their refusal to take personal responsibility for their team.

They may say their team is too timid, too lazy, too stupid, or too fill-in-the-blank…

They will tell you that if they just had a better team, they would be more successful. You can easily fall into making these kinds of excuses yourself. Don't. Because excuses like these are ignoring a fundamental truth…

There can be only one cause for a bad team. And that is a bad leader.

> *The cause usually comes down to someone who thinks they are not accountable, that they somehow get special rules applied to them. The truth is exactly the opposite.*

You have to model the behavior you want people to repeat. Be accountable yourself and always deliver what you promise. This type of integrity will greatly impact the culture of your team. Model the desired behaviors in areas like:

- Recruiting
- Rank advancement
- Integrity
- Productivity

If you're not willing to do this, you're in the wrong business.

Hold your people responsible as well. In a loving way, call them on their sh... stuff.

Operate with Integrity

This is related to the last item but deserves its own mention. People are seldom influenced (at least not consciously) by those they don't trust. Whenever I enroll someone into my business, I make two pledges to them:

1. I will never knowingly lie to them.
2. I will never knowingly tell them anything that isn't in the best interest of their business.

I suggest you adopt the same approach. If people don't trust you, you're going to have a difficult time influencing them in a positive way.

Be a Facilitator

Don't do everything yourself. Involve the team and get everyone participating.

One of the philosophies I follow for my business is to never do anything for people they are capable of doing themselves. Otherwise, you're weakening them, not helping them.

Don't Threaten People's Financial Security

There are way too many people being encouraged to quit their jobs too early. Many people are eager to leave their job as soon as they are making a few thousand dollars or euros a month. This is a bad idea and creates a great deal of unnecessary and damaging stress.

Your people will be much better served if, instead of trying to live out of that new income, they keep their job and reinvest their commissions in building additional lines.

Remember that most people are broke now. So if they trade their $40,000-a-year job for their $40,000-a-year Leveraged Sales business, they're still broke.

Encourage them to start paying down their credit cards, pay off their car loan, and have some investments building their net worth.

After they are debt-free, except perhaps for their mortgage, and earning more than they ever did in their job—only then is the time you can encourage them to quit their job and go full-time with the business.

Give Assignments

No matter the platform—local training seminar, major event, webcast, or the annual convention—one of the most powerful growth strategies is to give people homework to complete. The more these are specific action steps, the better. (Examples: Invite 15 people to view the next live-streaming presentation, find an accountability partner before they leave the event, plan their campaign for the next major event, etc.)

Lead the People—Manage Their Conflicts

I hate to even type these words. But I would be remiss if I did not. To become a strong leader in Leveraged Sales, you're going to need to become a conflict resolution expert. The biggest challenges you'll ever face are the people issues.

I remember doing a leadership symposium at the Mastermind Event one year. Someone asked me what a typical day of work was like for me. Here's what I said:

"Right now I have one top leader who isn't speaking to me because I didn't put him on the platform for the last event, since he hasn't rank advanced in three years and his volume is decreasing, not increasing. Another leader is furious with me, because I gave her only 20 minutes of stage time at the last event while another leader got 25. One of my top distributorships is going through a divorce right now and they're battling over who is going to keep the business. And I have another leader I have to remove from all team responsibilities because he's having an affair with the wife of someone on his third level. Other than that, everything's peachy!"

I wasn't doing a comedy set. Everything I said was happening at that moment. Did I mention that the biggest challenges you'll ever face are the people issues?

A big part of your job will be making people dial down their emotions, check their egos, and handle differences like an adult. When someone calls you with a personality conflict, this is how you need to handle the situation:

> **Them:** "I have a big problem with Steve. Don't tell him I called you, but…"

> **You:** "Sorry to interrupt. If you have a problem with Steve, we need to get him on the call right now. Hang on while I see if he's available."

> **Them:** "No, no, no! I don't want him to know that I'm the one who complained."
> **You:** "Sorry, I never talk about someone else when they're not present. If we really want to solve this problem, we are going to have to handle this like adults. We need to get the three of us on the phone together and discuss the issues openly."

When you handle situations like that, your team understands that you don't play games or deal in gossip. Your deliberate action kills the organizational politics, thus creating an environment where issues can be resolved.

Challenge People

Way too many leaders and influencers are pandering to their people—patronizing them for playing small and safe.

Don't let yourself take that path.

Destroy complacency. Blow up comfort zones. Create a culture where people must increase their pace and be a little breathless to keep up.

Act as a catalyst to inspire them to become the highest possible version of themselves. There can be no greater gift and no greater honor than this.

Now you know the truth about becoming a leader. Where do you go from here? You need to build belief in your team. Not a belief in *you* but a belief in *them*. Which is where we will go next…

CHAPTER 15

Building Belief in Your Team

Hopefully, you've read my earlier book, *Making the First Circle Work*. (If not, please make some time to do that soon.) The entire book is devoted to the concept of transforming hope into belief. If you desire to become a powerful, beneficial leader, you need to become an expert at helping your team to do just that. Because...

> *Hope is what gets people into the business.*
>
> *Belief is what keeps people in the business.*

When someone joins the business or is still relatively new, they hope the business will work, they'll win a free trip, or they'll qualify for a bonus car.

When they get "over the line," that hope has transformed into belief. Now they don't *hope* the business will work or hope they will be successful. They *know* they will become successful. Because they have developed rock-solid belief.

How do you get your people over that line so they transition from hope to belief and become strong, productive members of your team? Allow me to share seven elements that I believe are necessary for the process. These aren't really skills. Some are habits. Some simply reflect a mindset. And some are techniques.

Each of these elements serves two purposes: making you a stronger leader and building belief in the people who follow you. Let's start with the list, then study each in greater detail.

1. Posture

2. Image

3. Events

4. Personal development

5. Consistency

6. Commitment

7. Sacrifice

1. POSTURE

Posture is a critical element in your prospecting process, and just as important while working with your team. Posture is a combination of what you believe, how you act, and the confidence you have. And most relevant to this discussion—the confidence you instill in others.

People who are over the line have posture. Those who are not over the line lack it. Posture is about knowing what you really have. You approach people with confidence, because you have no doubts in what you are offering to them.

When you don't have posture, you approach candidates (and the business as a whole) with mindsets like:

- I'll give this a try.
- I hope I don't get rejected.
- Let me see if any of my friends get excited first.

When you have posture, you approach with mindsets like:

- I'm going to crush this thing!
- Who can I offer this thermo-freakin'-amazing opportunity to?
- Who's next?

People with posture don't go after the easy people who are so desperate for income that they will join anything. They immediately approach the most busy, ambitious, successful people they know. And they approach them with a confident expectation of a positive outcome.

People over the line know that Leveraged Sales is a dream business. Really. That's not fluffy marketing prose. The business truly is a dream come true for millions of people. Look at the advantages and kinds of benefits someone can receive from it:

- Extremely low investment
- High profit potential
- Lifestyle benefits
- Lucrative tax breaks
- Opportunities for contribution
- No employee headaches
- Low stress
- Travel opportunities
- Residual income potential
- Passive income potential

So when you think about people you will approach, look for successful people who understand business. Then approach those people with posture. Don't chase after them or beg and plead for an audience. Confidently offer them the opportunity to get involved with something extraordinary. Something you know is probably superior to the job or business that person currently has.

The other thing that comes from posture is the ability to recruit up. Here's what I mean. When I joined my company, I did exactly as we just talked about. I went to the most busy, ambitious, successful people I knew. I let them know how big the opportunity was, and how big they could be in it.

There were about 10 people I felt could produce a multi-million-dollar business. (By the way, of those 10, seven had no Leveraged Sales experience. Yet I was confident they could earn that kind of money because they were intelligent and possessed both influence and good teaching skills.)

Now here is the key…

I've made millions of dollars in this business. But when I started talking to these people, I wasn't even a manager and hadn't even cashed my first $500 bonus check!

Do you really get that?

I didn't wait until I was earning six figures a month to project how big those people could be. I knew what I had and I presented the opportunity accordingly.

Playing small is not serving you. Being conservative is not serving you. And waiting for success before you approach the really successful people is not serving you.

A Stradivarius violin is worth millions even if you don't know how to play the violin. A Bugatti is still ferocious, whether or not you know how to drive. And Leveraged Sales is still one of the top ways in the world for someone with no experience, little capital, or a limited education to create true financial freedom.

Even if you just started the business yesterday and haven't made $20 yet, that does not diminish or restrict the potential the business has for your candidates. You have one of the finest business opportunities in the world. Start acting congruently. And that means with posture.

Go after people who make more money than you do, people who have more education than you do, and people who have reached higher levels of success than you have. You'll be pleasantly surprised to discover that they are a receptive, attentive, and open-minded audience.

Wear the six decades this business has been helping people as your breastplate. Hold the experience of your sponsorship line as your shield. Arm yourself with the confidence that the business has helped hundreds of thousands live a better life. (Then, pick up your cell phone—right now—and call the toughest candidate on your list. And speak with posture!)

2. IMAGE MATTERS

Mention this topic, and most people think they know what you mean. Most think their image is good. Most would be wrong.

Think about this…

Where do you first run into your candidates? Not at your business briefings or company events. Not even when you're prospecting. You will meet the vast majority of your candidates for the first time as you're going through your day-to-day life.

Okay, maybe you get all dolled up in a suit when you meet them at your business briefing. But by the time your candidate arrives at the briefing, their impression of you is already set. And in most cases this was determined by the first time they met you, most likely when you:

Went to a movie…

Shopped at the market…

Dropped in at a party…

Attended a concert or cultural event...

Got your car washed...

Met new people at a neighborhood BBQ...

In other words, while you are living your day-to-day life—standing on the sidelines at your kid's soccer game, picking up clothes from the dry cleaner, and shopping at the local mall—that's when you are going to first encounter many of your candidates. Or more accurately, they will encounter you.

So how do you look?

Do you look like the rank you want to be when you leave the house each day? Or do you look like a lot of people today who wear Budweiser T-shirts when they appear in court and workout gear to attend a wedding?

This doesn't mean you need to be wearing a Tom Ford suit every time you leave the house. But you have to look *sharp*. You can still look chic dressed in blue jeans if you're dressing on purpose.

Are your clothes pressed? Clean? Your breath is fresh? Hair styled? Appropriate jewelry?

And what about your attitude? Are you positive, friendly, and the kind of person people like to be around? Do you practice good manners and treat others with courtesy?

I remember visiting a city to meet a colleague who was seeking business from me. He picked me up at the airport and wined and dined me to show how important I was to him. But I found I didn't really like him and decided not to give him my business. You know why?

Because, although he treated me with respect, he didn't do that for anyone else. When we went through the tollbooth on the way from the airport, he didn't say a single word to the toll taker, not even hello. He just thrust a bill at him, waited for the change, and then drove off. I thought that was very rude.

The same thing happened at the restaurant. He treated me like a king but treated the waiter like garbage. I certainly doubted the sincerity of his respect toward me, and I was uncomfortable being around someone with so little regard for the dignity of others.

Every time you leave the house, you're projecting an image of yourself. Is the image you project one that would attract people to work in your business? Or repel them?

And then there's the second part…

The image you have among your group. Your team has a perception of you. This perception is based on factors like:

- How you speak
- The way you dress
- Your overall style
- How you treat others
- The skillsets you have developed
- Your rank and income
- Your personal brand

We spent a whole chapter on personal branding earlier, so I won't go into how you do that. But here are some additional thoughts on how your team's perception of you can be influenced.

One of the unique elements of the training events I hold for my top leaders is booking outside experts in image and etiquette. The truth is, most people who join our business have no idea about manners and etiquette (I sure didn't), because our society has gotten away from them. And many more people have no idea about fashion or style.

If you're a man and you fail to pull out the chair for a lady dining next to you, or let a door slam in her face, frankly you're a bore. And you're hardly going to impress candidates at a net-working lunch if you are pushing food onto your fork with your fingers, slurping your soup, or talking with food in your mouth. (Or have to ask them which bread plate or iced tea is yours.) An etiquette coach will do wonders for your image. Not to mention your confidence and self-esteem.

I see many women in the business who don't know how to put on makeup properly, wear enough perfume to stun an ox, or don't realize that a slinky dress that works for a dinner date might not be appropriate in a business context.

When I bought my first dress shirt, it didn't have any buttons on the sleeves. Instead it had these really cool cuffs with colorful plastic tabs that held the two sides together. Only after I wore it did someone inform me that those were called French cuffs and I was supposed to use cufflinks in those slots. I had no idea there even was such a thing as cufflinks in the world. (I also didn't realize that the brand label sewn on the outside of my first sports jacket was supposed to be removed. And the bargain outlet store where I bought it didn't tell me.)

Gentlemen: You look absolutely fabulous in that lavender, extended-length, six-button suit jacket. As long as you're performing at the Grammys with Dr. Hook or Kool & the Gang. If you're conducting a business presentation... not so much.

Often people have a hairstyle that's way out of date or doesn't flatter their features. Did you know that if you have a round face, you should wear square glasses? And if you have a square face, wear round ones. It balances the look to make you more attractive. If you have an ample butt, wearing a jacket with side vents will make the back flap jut out. You'll look better in a jacket with no vents.

How many people know tips like these? I sure didn't. An image makeover by a good professional can boost your self-confidence and produce remarkable growth for your career.

In this business, you're always selling the dream. You sell the dream to candidates with your presentations. And you're selling the dream to your team by how you live. The image you project determines whether or not a candidate joins your team. In fact, your image often determines whether they will even review your information or attend your meeting.

Even when you're brand new in the business, you can project an image of confidence, belief, and professionalism. And nothing will attract good candidates faster than an image like that.

The image you have with your team will dramatically affect how far you can go and how fast you get there. Is your image that of a leader or a follower? Do you project trust or create doubt? Do you look like a professional or an amateur? Give some real thought to the image you project and grade yourself—critically and honestly—in this category.

3. BUILDING THROUGH EVENTS

Getting someone over the line means helping him or her to develop a "no turning back" mindset. They have a rock-solid commitment to the business and your company and will not quit, no matter what challenges present themselves.

They are *in*. They are so in that it won't matter if:

- All the products are on backorder for six weeks
- Their top leader quits
- The company is the recipient of negative publicity on national television
- Their cousin Pookie insists that the business won't work

None of those situations will matter because they are over the line. Because they have belief, not hope.

And nothing gets people over the line better than major events…

They are the glue that holds the organization together and the vehicle for critical functions such as recognition and training. They're also the best medium for building belief. In a way that can't be replicated through any other means.

If you are not in charge of events, you might think this category doesn't apply to you. That would be a mistake. Because the real issue here is how you promote and use the events available to you. Many will be events from your sponsorship line; others will be put on by the company. They might be generic events.

I do believe the best scenario is a steady diet of events put on by the field leadership and your company. These events will be the most helpful in terms of building belief in your specific company, product line, and system.

The most effective approach is having three or four major events a year, spaced out every three or four months.

(And an extra one, a leadership program, but only for high-level pin ranks, not for the whole team.) Usually, one of these is the annual convention hosted by the company.

Here is the thing you must understand if you want to be a leader and continually grow your network...

You have to be at every one of these events. But most of them are not designed for you. They are designed for your team—to get them over the line. Your role is to create a culture where the events and attendance at them is a top priority.

You must promote every event and get as many of your team members there as possible. Let's suppose you get 25 people at a major event. If the event is done right, at least 10 of them will get over the line. Something will happen that clicks, and they'll "get it."

This transformation can be created by a multitude of different possibilities during major events: By meeting the company president and looking in her eyes. Or watching a speech from one of the top income earners. Or because of a comment from the person sitting next to them. Or maybe just a conversation that happens in the hallway during a break. Often this alteration occurs when someone is giving their acceptance speech for reaching a new rank. A certain number of your people will relate to that person and realize that the story they are hearing could be their story.

They resolve to make that story true for themselves. And once that happens, game over. They will make it come true, because now they are over the line.

There's a good chance that 15 of your 25 may not have this aha moment. But at the very least, they'll be excited, leave a little more motivated, and probably move into increased action. Some of them will then come back to the next event and get over the line there. Or the one after that.

Some will have to come to 5, 10, or even 15 events before they get over the line. Others will never get over the line and will drop out along the way. But they will be replaced and the team augmented by the new recruits brought in from the people who got over the line.

The Magic of 100

Once you get at least 100 distributorships (a husband and wife would count as one distributorship) from your team to an event—you cross a tipping point. Having at least 100 business centers represented ensures you have enough leaders who will stick around and eventually get over the line. Then true duplication sets in and your business is vested.

So the secret to success starts with getting to your first major event. Bring as many of your team members with you as you can. Learn to *promote* events, not just *announce* them. Create a culture where event attendance is standard operating procedure.

> *There are five reasons we conduct major events. And everyone—and I do mean everyone—is always in need of one of those five results.*

They are:

1. To gain knowledge
2. To improve attitude
3. To change behavior
4. To develop skills
5. To build belief

After you reach a certain point, the events are not really about you learning skillsets. (With the exception of an annual Leadership Summit, which is focused on helping you develop your leadership skills.) The events are there for you to use to build your team faster.

The most successful leaders in our profession are experts who build from major event to major event. And that's what you must do.

In an interview, I was asked to describe the essence of the business for leaders. I replied that the true essence of the business is selling two items, and two items only:

1. Your products
2. Tickets to the next major event

Period. End of story.

Now you might ask, "What about selling the dream?" That happens at the major events. You might ask about training people in skillsets. That happens at the major events. In fact, all of the critical skills in which your team needs training or belief-building happen at the major events. That's why you have to make promoting from major event to major event a linchpin of your strategy.

4. Personal Development

This is the most important daily habit to have in the business, and the one that most new people resist. Because telling people they need to work on themselves isn't sexy. To them, the sexy thing is learning more prospecting techniques. What they fail to understand is this:

> *If you aren't the kind of person people trust, believe in, and want to work with, they'll never join your business.*

The other issue is that to be successful in the business, you have to have a certain confidence, demeanor, and presence. And that comes from who you are—and that begins with personal development.

If you remember, the first element was posture. You can't have good posture if you don't have the right mindset. And personal development is going to be the biggest influence to create your mindset.

The fact is, our business is not easy. Simple, but not easy. Sometimes we're approaching skeptical people who don't always understand the differences between sketchy money games and legitimate Leveraged Sales. Often we are promoting breakthrough products that need some explanation. We're bringing in a lot of people who never have been their own boss before, so turnover is a reality of the process. We have to have positive energy all the time.

You have to see challenges as growth opportunities, setbacks as learning experiences, and adversity as necessary for character building. And that's pretty tough to do when you are surrounded by negativity all day as many of us are.

The truth is, most of your average coworkers, friends, and family members are probably negative. They don't mean to be, but they can't help themselves. They're being programmed—

24 hours a day, seven days a week—just as you are. (If you want an extremely deep dive into all of the mind viruses you are being programmed with, read my book *Why You're Dumb, Sick, and Broke... and How to Get Smart, Healthy, and Rich!*)

To really have a positive mindset, you have to counter-program your subconscious mind with positive programming. Every great leader in our business does this religiously, usually on a daily basis.

I believe in 30 minutes of daily self-development time, done first thing in the morning. Doing this early creates your consciousness and determines the results you will get that day.

For some reason, most new people think top leaders never have anyone quit on them, never face any adversity, or all candidates say yes. The truth is top leaders face a lot *more* challenges, adversity, and rejection. But they spend enough personal development time so these setbacks don't prevent them from reaching success. They are so far over the line it wouldn't matter if an earthquake swallowed up the corporate headquarters. They'll still find a way to be successful and they'll never quit.

Success is not a physical destination but an ongoing journey of mental equilibrium. Top leaders work on themselves daily to keep their psychological state positive enough that the negative outcomes can never outweigh the positive ones.

That's where you need to be...

Sustained success isn't just about getting you over the line or keeping you from quitting. It is about dramatically improving the results you produce, each and every day. Personal development time in the morning creates a change in your physiological state, which in turn produces better outcomes and results from the actions you take that day.

If you call 10 people and invite them to a presentation, you will have a certain result. I promise that you will achieve a better result if you spent some time that morning listening to my *Power Prosperity Podcast*.

If you read the book *As a Man Thinketh* for 15 minutes when you wake up, you will be a different person at your presentation or training event that night. There will be a different posture in your body, a different tone in your voice, and a different look in your eyes. And that translates into real results.

5. HOW CONSISTENT ARE YOU?

Consistency may not sound as enticing as a hot new social media marketing technique. But consistency will make you rich in Leveraged Sales. In fact, the single biggest disparity between the top earners and the grinders is how they approach consistency.

If I asked you whether you're consistent, you would probably assure me that you are. Most people believe this. But most people are not even close to being consistent in their business efforts.

For my group, we do a leadership webcast once a week. Many new team members listen the first couple of weeks. Then life gets in the way. The successful leaders are on 50 times a year. They're consistent.

The same thing happens with opportunity presentations and training events. Most people start off with strong participation. But suddenly urgent events—like having to mow the lawn, help a friend move a sofa, or the in-laws coming to town—become a valid excuse to neglect their business. Consistency means consistency.

Most people don't need bigger goals, but better daily habits.

6. WHAT'S YOUR LEVEL OF COMMITMENT?

Being committed sounds easy, right? Isn't everybody?

Hardly.

The vast majority of the people in the business enter with a provisional commitment at best. They utter statements like, "I'll give this a try."

They have a commitment to success—provided that commitment doesn't inconvenience them, interfere with their comfort zone routine, or conflict with their favorite TV shows.

Commitment is like principle. You don't really know you have it until you're tested.

Commitment is not jogging every day—except when it rains. Commitment means you get wet or you move your run to the fire escape stairway. Rain or shine, you're committed.

Some frequent advice you'll hear is: Treat your business like a business. Here's what's better: Treat your business like a job.

Why?

People are committed to jobs, because otherwise they get passed up for promotions, miss raises, or get fired. You don't miss work when the *American Idol* finale is on, you move, or *The Lion King* comes to town. Your business commitment should be the same way.

Here are two important commitments that will make a real difference for your business:

1. Commit to working your business at least 10 to 15 hours a week.

2. Commit to working your business for at least one year.

We've already discussed both of these items, so I won't belabor them. But how many people literally work at least 10 hours a week? And, more importantly, do you?

Watching the corporate video four more times during the week is not doing the business. Scrolling through your back office to see how often the volume goes up is not doing the business. And perusing your Facebook feed isn't either.

Doing the business is actively retailing, prospecting, and presenting. Or helping someone on your team to actively retail, prospect, or present. Those are the "rainmaker" activities that spur growth and produce income. So you want to devote as many of your 10 to 15 hours a week to them as possible.

We discussed making that commitment for your first year. Yet how many people drop out in their first two weeks? How many give up after two months? How many times have you been involved in this business in the past and quit before a year was up?

Truth is, Leveraged Sales is a two- to four-year plan for most people to reach sustainable, serious income. People do not get rich in four or six months. It takes time to locate key leaders, get them trained, and build the proper infrastructure. Unless you're rolling over a bunch of people from some other company, there are no shortcuts to that.

I recognize that a two- to four-year commitment might seem like a long time to you. But what about the 45 or 55 years you'll end up spending in a series of "normal" jobs? And if you follow the job path, where will you be financially at the end of those four or five *decades?*

So are you all in for that first year? What did you really do for your 10 or 15 hours last week? What do you have scheduled this week? Give that some serious thought.

7. SACRIFICE

I already told you *sacrifice* is the last item on the list.

And this one may have surprised you. After all, telling a candidate or even a team member they have to sacrifice is neither compelling nor enticing. We recruit all the time on money, lifestyle, and luxury. And Leveraged Sales does offer all those benefits. But not to start.

To begin and build something big—you're going to have to sacrifice.

You and everyone you bring into the business are already using all 24 hours of every day. Using them to perform certain daily habits in certain ways. Ways that most likely keep you in your comfort zone.

That means to obtain those 10 to 15 hours a week to do the business, you'll have to sacrifice whatever you are now doing during that time.

This sacrifice doesn't have to last forever. But you will need to sacrifice at the start. I became the number one income earner worldwide in a company only because I was willing to sacrifice.

Most people see every blockbuster movie the week it's released. They watch at least 10 TV shows weekly. I missed most of those or caught them on plane rides a couple months later. My top leaders took more spa days, cruises, and vacations than I ever did. But I made the decision to sacrifice in the early years to ultimately achieve more in the future.

Don't get me wrong…

I still did the stuff that brings me great joy. I would go to the midnight preview of a *Star Wars* movie or opening night at the Met, and I had no compunction about turning down a $50,000 speech that conflicted with my softball playoffs. When there was something I was passionate about, I found a way to savor it. But I kept a relentless mindset about making sacrifices that provided a huge return on investment for my future. My mantra was:

> *I will do today what others will not, so later I can do what others cannot.*

And you know what? That mantra worked for me. And will for you as well.

Are you making the sacrifices today that will bring you true freedom tomorrow? Or are you living in the moment of instant gratification—which will keep you in the grinder category forever?

Here's the list again:

1. Posture
2. Image
3. Events
4. Personal development
5. Consistency
6. Commitment
7. Sacrifice

These elements are what elite leaders do to build massive networks. (Sometimes consciously, sometimes instinctively.) The most successful ones employ all of them. Give some serious thought to evaluating yourself in all seven of the elements above. After an honest appraisal, you'll know better what areas you need work on.

The next step is learning how to recognize, discover, and develop leaders in your team. And that's what you'll learn in the next chapter…

CHAPTER 16

How to Create a Leadership Factory

How do you recognize potential leaders, nurture them, and then facilitate a process where they can continue that development of leaders—down hundreds or even thousands of levels in your organization?

You won't accomplish this through strength of personality, training longer, or sharing more motivational quotes in your WhatsApp groups.

You've got to create an institutional culture that values leadership, recognizes potential, and rewards results. And throw in a little celebration too. Let's unpack that process to analyze what good leaders look like, where they come from, and how they're developed.

Having built teams of more than 200,000 people, I've had a great vantage point from which to witness the leadership development process firsthand—starting with a talent pool of potential leaders and tracking the behavior patterns that cause them to develop into actual leaders. And one surprising discovery I've noticed is the huge disparity in the various origin stories of leaders in our profession.

There are kids who were raised in wealth and privilege and kids who grew up on the street. Kids who were raised in strong traditional families and kids with no family to speak of. Pampered kids with helicopter parents and kids who were abused.

At the time distributors reach your team, they could be Fortune 500 CEOs, homemakers, or gangbangers. Schoolteachers, serial entrepreneurs, or Uber drivers. There is no template from people's past that determines their probability of success in our profession. Everyone on your candidate list has the possibility and potential to become your next successful leader.

So what are the commonalities that define those who do succeed at becoming strong, positive leaders?

The primary commonality is they *decided* to become a leader.

Your background defines you only if you allow it to. You decide whether to stay on the track you're on or change the course. The people who become successful leaders at some point make the decision to become a leader. They don't waste time trying to "find" themselves. They decide the kind of person they want to become, and then they create that person.

They decide to learn new skills, work on themselves, and take the actions. They decide to schedule their working hours, prioritize their actions, and conduct the presentations. A huge dynamic is deciding to hold themselves accountable. And, perhaps most importantly, they decide they are worthy of a leadership position.

Once you make that decision, your perspective changes radically. Instead of focusing on how you become more successful yourself, you start migrating toward ways to add value to the team.

If we put leadership under a microscope and break down the DNA, it's ultimately going to lead us to the essence—adding value. Adding more value to the team than you are taking from the team.

This is bigger than thinking about yourself, your customers, and your team members. To be a leader, you have to understand that you are an organism within a greater ecosystem—which includes not just your team, but also your sponsorship line, the system, the company, and even the other companies in the profession.

If you start drinking your own Kool-Aid, you begin to believe that everything revolves around you. Your overactive ego will suck too much oxygen out of the ecosystem and all the organisms suffer—even and especially you. You may think because you're the top dog, you're somehow immune to the laws of physics. You're not.

TEACHING OTHERS HOW TO THINK

Let's return to my definition of leadership, the part about inspiring people to become the highest possible version of themselves.

You can make this possible only when your team increases their belief and esteem as a result of their exposure to you. That means you have done much more than demonstrate leadership skills and qualities to them. *You have allowed them to imagine the possibility that they can achieve this same level of development in themselves.*

Strong, positive leaders do this by helping those who follow them believe in themselves. And a critical element in this is teaching them not *what* to think, but *how* to think.

The old leadership model was to teach people what to think. The belief was that if you simply indoctrinated people as to what to think (and one of those thoughts is to never question authority), they would blindly follow.

The fact is, many people are actively looking to be shown what to think. They search the globe for gurus to follow and movements to join. The strong presence today of gangs, cults, and even organized religion is a manifestation of this.

People watch networks like ESPN and BBC Sport to learn what they should think about their hometown team superstar. They listen to bombastic buffoons on talk-radio stations to know what to think about political issues. And they read the entertainment blogs so they can know who is hip, hot, and trendy.

The education system around the world is not teaching young people to think. It is forcing them to memorize facts to pass tests. The same facts they could look up in six seconds on their smartphone.

Although this environment exists, strong, positive leaders do not exploit it.

They carefully choose the people they lead and select only those who are interested in thinking for themselves. They create a climate in which people develop problem-solving skills, which cultivates thought and builds belief in themselves. (And not incidentally, considerably increases duplication.)

> *True leaders don't develop people's belief in the leader; they develop a belief in the follower.*

They foster growing confidence and esteem in their followers and help those people think independently. This free thinking and newfound confidence causes followers to empower themselves into leadership behaviors of their own. Leaders beget more leaders, the only real test of leadership.

INVESTING IN LEADERS

As I was flying home one night, the flight attendant came by my seat to thank me for my loyal business. She noted that I was a three-million-miler and said she didn't even know how that was humanly possible. (I didn't have the heart to tell her that I also have almost four million miles on other airlines.) This year I'm at the elite level on three different carriers. You know why I travel so much?

I'm investing in leaders.

Because I know that a well-trained leader in a Leveraged Sales organization is one of the most lucrative investments in the world. Time invested in a potential leader can pay off for decades. The best part is that your investment pays back in many ways other than the astonishing financial return. You will get to see a lot of other interesting places and cultivate wonderful, enriching friendships that add real value to your life.

I am always shocked by how many people in the business fail to invest in leaders. Especially long distance ones. It's sometimes frustrating how much prodding it takes to convince someone to get on a plane and work with their long distance lines.

So what about you?

Are you investing in your leaders? Grooming the leaders of tomorrow? If you want to create a leadership factory on your team, you're going to need to invest in discovering, developing, and training those leaders.

It could start with something as simple as giving a copy of this book to a promising new distributor. Sometimes it's driving four or five hours to work with someone in another town. And often it means getting on an airplane and flying halfway across the country, or around the world, to help develop a new leader.

Think of your business as a leadership conveyor belt. Your job every month is to churn out more leaders. And then teach those leaders how to churn out more of their own.

The great news is that once you do this, you are setting the example that will be duplicated in your group. And once you have really built this culture in your group, that's where true wealth is created.

FIVE FOUNDATIONAL PREMISES

Let me share five foundational premises about leadership in our particular business. I believe these premises qualify as First Principles on which everything else is built. Take a look at the list and then we'll break them down individually.

1. You're running an all-volunteer army.
2. If you ask everyone to lead, no one does.
3. Challenge, don't pander.

4. You must work three rungs in the ladder.

5. Recruiting leaders produces growth now—grooming leaders produces sustained growth.

Let's look at the first premise. I struggled mightily in my first tour of duty in the business. The second time around I was able to attract talented people much more easily, and I built much more quickly. Reflecting back on the differences between the two experiences, I believe my eventual success was due to what I had learned working with volunteer organizations in the meantime. (I had been the president of the Chamber of Commerce, my church board, and the Florida Speakers Association.)

Every volunteer organization is an all-volunteer army. There is no conscription and you can't hire and fire people. *You have to fashion an environment where they want to become a willing contributor.* And guess what? This is also exactly the case with leading a team of people in Leveraged Sales.

The second premise speaks to a frequent mistake new people make in the business. They assume everyone is a leader and give all of their people leadership metrics to perform. This mistake can kill your group fast.

They make statements to their team like, "Everyone here is a leader. So you have to [make cold calls until your fingers bleed, conduct 20 presentations a week, etc.]."

No, everyone is not a leader. Not everyone even wants to be a leader. In fact, a huge portion of your team will be people who joined explicitly to follow you or other leaders.

So when you make leadership activity a requirement for acceptance, you end up driving away a lot of good people. Some of the people you lose wouldn't have become leaders but still would be valuable members of your team. And others would have developed into leaders, but the speed you were demanding scared them away prematurely.

Some people who are followers turn out to be capable field generals. They will work relentlessly to implement and maintain systems, events, and policies in the organization. They're just not going to be helpful to you in designing them.

You need to be aware of your group dynamics—who is who on your team in their roles as:

A. Customers

B. Retailers

C. Casual Builders (Followers)

D. Serious Builders (Field generals)

E. Leaders

My third premise is about the need to challenge people. *People don't develop into the highest possible version of themselves if they are surrounded by people who give them permission to stay just as they are.* (Which is what almost everyone around them is doing now.) They need someone to challenge them to become more.

That someone needs to be you.

Let's look at the fourth premise and what I mean by working three rungs in the ladder. The activities that drive growth, like training and counseling, are always done across levels in the organization. The Bronze rank distributor is counseling with their up-line Silver rank, and that Silver is counseling with their up-line Gold rank distributor.

Both your progress as a leader—and your ability to nurture other leaders—are based on this dynamic. Make sure you are reaching down a level to help those below you. And also reaching up a level to receive assistance yourself. These leaders up-line are your best source of help. When you create partnerships with them, you are better equipped to guide and support those below you. And you are modeling the leadership traits that will develop more leaders in your group. (As they will duplicate the same process down the group.)

Let's dig deeper into the last premise. Too many people are chasing after leaders in other programs, trying to entice them jump ship. That can give you a quick volume boost. But to create viable long-term volume and duplication, you need to be grooming your leaders from within.

If you are intrigued by the idea of these five foundational premises, be sure to read my book *Lead Your Team*. It contains 21 leadership lessons for Direct Selling and really captures my philosophy on the topic. Now let's explore…

THE LEADERSHIP DEVELOPMENT PATH IN LEVERAGED SALES

1. Decide
2. Become proficient at the four basic skillsets (Meeting people, working a candidate list, inviting, followup)
3. Lead people who choose to follow (using the study, do, and teach simultaneously approach)
4. Become proficient at leadership skillsets (Presenting, people skills, leadership skills)
5. Identify and reach out to potential leaders
6. Train those aspiring leaders on the leadership skillsets
7. Train those aspiring leaders how to lead their followers
8. Lead the leaders (inspiration, vision, purpose)
9. Fire yourself

What I described above is how I would map out the path you take as you develop your skills in both the business and leadership. This subject is too important for a superficial overview or fluffy platitudes. So let's look in greater detail at some of the day-to-day activities being a leader in our business entails.

Follow the System

Great leaders know there is also a time to follow. Because leaders are strong-minded, this can sometimes be an issue. But following the system must remain sacred with you as a leader. If you change the system, even only slightly, you will send a message to the organization that it's okay to change the system. Then the next level does it too, and by four levels down, the system no longer exists.

Of course, from time to time, market conditions will dictate that the system needs to be modified. Let me give you an idea of how you might go about making a change if you need to do so...

Let's say you have reached the top-rank pin level in your company, you have five top-rank pin levels on your front line, and you're thinking about changing something in your system. Suppose you want to remove a book that you're using at a certain point of the sponsoring process and substitute another. (Like this one! 😬)

You place it on the agenda at your annual leadership conference or at another event that your top leaders attend. (In my case, the event was a Diamond Retreat—a weekend where each qualified Diamond Director paid their own way to attend. It was not an official company event, just a chance for the team Diamonds to plan long-term team strategy.) Next, you send everyone a copy of the new resource you're proposing prior to the event, so they can review it ahead of time. Then at the event, you discuss and reach a consensus.

The system should be changed only from the inside as an entire organization. When you make a change in this way, it protects the integrity of the system. Then the system protects the integrity of your residual income.

Monthly Counseling

This is the monthly process you perform with the people you enroll in your organization to keep them growing on a consistent basis. (I realize that many of you are probably in a weekly pay plan. But I think counseling becomes unmanageable if attempted weekly and works best if done once a month, regardless of pay frequency.)

Here's how counseling works.

Let's say you're a Bronze Director with your company and the next rank up is Silver Director. You would counsel with the first Silver Director in your sponsorship line. Now, once you become a Silver Director, if your sponsor is still a Silver Director, you would no longer counsel with her. Instead, you would go to her sponsor, who is a Gold Director.

You always counsel with the next up-line person who is qualified at the rank above yours. (If you want to know how to be a Gold Director, you have to talk to somebody who has already reached that level. If you want to be a Diamond Director, you need to be counseled by a Diamond Director.)

This ensures that everyone has someone to counsel with, and also that the top ranks don't have thousands of people looking to them for counseling. Just like the sponsorship lines work, you work with your front-line leaders, who work with their front-line leaders, who work with their front-line leaders. In the event you're in a sponsorship line with a person or two at the same rank as you—go up the organization to find someone who will be willing to work with you.

It should be noted that just because your sponsor is the same rank as you does not mean that they are a bad leader or don't know the business.

It simply means that they have helped you achieve fast growth. As quite often happens, your sponsor brought people up to their own rank slightly before they moved up a rank themselves. So don't judge them negatively or hold that against them.

Celebrate the fact that they helped you get this far and counsel with the appropriate person in your sponsorship line.

Learn from their experience. They will already have made the same mistakes you are headed toward, which means they can cut many years off your learning curve. Be open-minded and coachable, because they have a vested interest in your success.

One other note on this: In new organizations, particularly fast-growing ones, these lines are going to get blurred sometimes. You might have 60, 80, even 100 new members join your team that month, and none of them have really had any time to solidify their rank and learn how to coach those below them. Trust me, this is a great problem to have. You deal with it by having higher rank leaders do more group counseling. It's a little messy, but it still works and will crystallize better as your team matures.

A counseling session can help you only if it is based in reality. The person you are counseling with needs accurate information to work with. Don't draw out 12 lines if you really have only five active lines. Don't tell them you invited 15 people to the presentation when you really invited only three. Otherwise, the counseling is based on faulty premises and the advice you receive won't really help you.

In terms of the actual counseling, the foundation is tracking the key metrics each session. Here are the ones I think are the most important (your sponsorship line may have others):

- Rank
- Personal volume
- Number of distributors in the team
- Total team volume
- Average volume per distributor
- Number of retail customers
- Average customer volume
- Number of new enrollments

- Number of personal active lines
- Number of personal lines with a leader
- Total leaders in the team

It should be self-explanatory why these particular metrics are important. You always want to know if they're moving in the right direction. By analyzing them you can predict where someone's check is going to be three months from now with a shocking degree of accuracy. (Once you know how to assess the metrics.)

Early on, the most important metrics are the amount of customers, average customer volume, and new enrollments. As a team starts to develop, the lines with a leader and total number of leaders in the team will gain in importance. Because these metrics determine the future growth. We know that a line can have 20 people in it, but if none of them are leaders—within three months it will probably be greatly reduced or gone entirely.

We can have another line with only two people in it, but if they're both leaders, that line may have 40 or 50 people a month later. Leaders produce leaders. So pay more attention to the leadership metrics as your people's teams grow.

It's important that every month you counsel with your people, collect and aggregate the data, then send it to the person you will counsel with.

Dealing with Mistakes from On High

I hate to break this news to you, but there will be times when your company or sponsorship line is going to mess up. Not because they're necessarily bad people, but because all companies and sponsorship lines make mistakes at some point. Get used to it.

The company may launch with a bad comp plan or change the plan and it doesn't perform as projected. The distributors struggle, lose faith, and quit.

Or the sponsorship line acts out of integrity by taking some action that harms the team. Members of the team feel betrayed, lose faith, and quit.

That's the superficial assessment. But here's what really happens in those cases…

Yes the company or sponsorship line screwed up and caused the problem. But the distributors didn't quit because they lost faith in the company or sponsorship line. They quit because they lost faith in themselves.

Whether your people lose faith or stay confident will be mostly affected by how the leadership responds when these challenges occur. The sacred rule of our business is that negativity *never, never, never* goes down the group. Any time something bad happens and you want to complain about it, call the company or someone up the sponsorship line. But never commiserate with your team about it unless you want to drive them away.

Sometimes the situation becomes severe. The company or leadership is continually making serious mistakes, not learning from those mistakes, or showing bad faith. You reach an untenable state where you feel you can no longer maintain a positive face with your team. In that case, you have no alternative but to resign and look for another company where you can build while maintaining your integrity.

Structuring Events

Your event structure is a powerful ally in developing new generations of leaders. Think of the event levels as a farm system, similar to what major sports do. Baseball has the minor leagues, American basketball has a development league, and most national soccer teams have youth divisions that they draw their talent from. Utilize your event structure the same way.

People begin with doing a 30-second testimonial at a local meeting or broadcast. Then they might graduate to giving a five-minute presentation. Later they are doing keynotes or train-ing sessions at regional events. And ultimately, they may be on the stage at a national convention or worldwide webcast. As they develop their presentation skills and continue to rank advance, their visibility should increase.

It's very important that you vet people for these roles carefully…

The most sacred position in your organization is being on the platform in front of your team. By "platform" I mean on the stage at physical events, appearing on conference calls or web-casts, and being featured in marketing materials. There is an implied endorsement of people you allow on the platform, so it is important to consider these people mindfully.

The first requirement for platform consideration should be that the person is someone who has already built a successful business or is moving quickly in the process of building a big business.

It's also important that the person be a team player and following the system. If you have someone up on the platform teaching strategies that are off-system—that will negatively influence your group and hinder your leadership development.

Loyalty and consistency are important traits. You don't want to edify someone onstage at the March meeting, only to have people hear that they quit and joined another opportunity in April. If you believe someone is a flight risk, keep them off the platform.

Another issue has developed in the last two decades you should be aware of: the cottage industry of parasites that feed off of our profession. Every motivational speaker, seminar leader, consultant, coach, and guru sees the huge crowds of enthusiastic people at our conventions and begins salivating at the idea of selling to us.

Some of these people are well meaning and helpful. As I men-tioned, I've brought in etiquette and fashion consultants to work with my elite leaders in the past. I also hired a brilliant branding consultant to work with us on developing our message for use in marketing materials. It's essential that, when designing a compensation plan, every company engage a competent professional compensation consultant. Just as important is to keep a law firm on retainer that specializes in Direct Selling.

Bringing in a powerful motivational speaker to conduct an inspirational opening or closing keynote can provide astonishing value to your convention or major event. But you must be mindful and work with them on their content to ensure their message is empowering and doesn't create conflict with your system.

Some of these people are well meaning—yet NOT helpful. There are legions of sales trainers, NLP coaches, and marketing consultants who do not understand the unique dynamics of our business. If you bring them in, they can teach techniques and strategies that instead of increasing duplication actually kill it.

Some of these people are NOT well meaning—and, surprise, NOT helpful. Simply put, they're only on a money grab. They are often distributors from other companies who want access to your people so they can steal them away. Or they might be someone who bought a successful distributorship, or inherited it from their parents, and they haven't got a clue about how to build a business themselves. Most often they are distributors who have washed out of the business and now support themselves selling crap to your team.

Have a Defined Leadership Track

To truly create a leadership factory, your people need to know what the pathway for becoming a leader with the team looks like. If you're a new recruit in the Navy and your dream is to become an Admiral, you have an idea of what all the ranks leading up to the Admiralty are and what the responsibilities of each are. Your team needs to create a similar scenario. Your new recruits need to know what ranks, behaviors, and team activities put them on the path of becoming a leader with the team. (You'll see an excellent example of this in the levels of leadership described below.)

Impose the Death Penalty Where Appropriate

If your company reaches critical mass and starts experiencing exponential growth, you're going to witness the next zombie apocalypse. At any given moment, there are thousands of MLM Zombies desperately looking for a new hot deal, because the last money game or "under the table" deal they had collapsed.

Unfortunately, in this group, there are at least 30 or 40 people who have done such a deceitful job promoting themselves, they are actually thought of as veteran leaders by some. They often maintain a strong presence on social media, consult to gullible start-up companies, or conduct generic seminars in the space.

They will come into your company and make a big splash with all the rollover zombies they bring with them. But once they stall out or someone offers them a deal somewhere else, they'll bolt and try to take as many of your people with them as they can.

Likewise, you have to be alert for "terrorists," the people who act illegally, steal recruits, or flout the policies and procedures. This unethical behavior destroys the culture in your organization and can even threaten the viability of the company.

Above all else, you must protect your organization. So when people reveal that they are zombies or terrorists, impose the death penalty: immediate termination. Do this swiftly and publicly, so people understand what is and isn't accepted in your culture.

One of the best practices that intrigues me comes from companies in other industries: the "panic button." Often this really is a big red physical button, other times it's just a process to follow.

In either case, any member of the team is authorized to push the button at any time without negative consequences.

An example would be a manufacturing plant with a conveyor belt. If something happens that could put workers in danger or create a substandard product, any worker can stop production so the situation can be evaluated.

Another great example of this is Cirque du Soleil. Each live show has a stage director in charge of the action. If the director sees *any* cast member—a trapeze artist, stagehand, or even an usher—cross their arms in front of their chest—the lights come up, the music ends, and the show stops instantly. Those crossed arms are the panic button sign, which could mean a safety mat is out of place, a piece of equipment isn't anchored right, or a toddler wandered into a dangerous area. Any Cirque employee is empowered to give the sign if they feel anyone is in danger.

I believe every great organization should have this type of panic button process in place. (Think how much sooner the #MeToo movement could have advanced if organizations had this type of system earlier.) It's important that we police ourselves. So if a distributor is manipulating the back office of someone else in their team, making social media posts claiming cancer cures, front-loading new members, or doing anything that threatens the team or company—people must be encouraged and empowered to speak up without fear of retribution. It will do wonders to keep the terrorists and zombies in check.

THE FOUR LEVELS OF LEADERSHIP

You've seen what a delineated leadership track looks like and the important behaviors that develop leaders along that track. Now I would like to share something very special with you: My own personal criteria I use to evaluate leaders. These can provide you with powerful insights into creating that conveyor belt of leaders on your team.

Here's how the levels break down:

Level One Leader

- Solid personal use of the products themselves.
- Has developed a strong customer base.
- Proficient in the four basic skillsets.
- Promotes using third-party tools and system, not personality.
- Attends major events.
- Builds depth with the team.
- Volunteers with team events and projects.

Level Two Leader

- All of the above.
- Is in the ticket-selling business, promoting major events.
- Reached a "threshold" (serious) rank.
- Investing in long distance lines.
- Working the business 15–20 hours a week for transition.
- Starting to appear on the platform locally.

Level Three

- All of the above.
- Active in tap-rooting lines.
- Has built at least six strong long distance lines.
- Full-time in the business.
- Reached an elite rank.
- On the platform for major events.
- Leadership duplication happening on their team.
- A "big kid." They kill distractions, resolve conflicts, and are self-disciplined.

Level Four

- All of the above.

- A strategic thinker. Someone who can participate in the design and implementation of training curriculum, system development, and culture.

- Understands the big picture. Can be a valuable stakeholder with the company, perhaps serve on the advisory board. Able to recognize the need for policies or processes that may not always be popular with the field but are necessary for the health of the company.

- A maestro who brings out the unique and best talents of each member of the orchestra.

As you can see, this definition of leadership is glaringly different from what most people in our business understand it to be. In a team of 100,000 people, in your first five years, you likely won't have more than one to four people who would actually qualify as a level four leader.

Here's the most important thing you must know about these levels: You have to adapt your coaching to interact one level up from the person you are working with.

For example, let's suppose you are a level four leader, and you've just sponsored a new enrollee. You can't be relating to them from up in the clouds as a level four leader. In their case, you need to serve their needs by acting as a level one leader with them. When they develop into a level one leader, you interact with them as a level two leader. Only with your level three leaders do you interact as a level four leader.

Level four leaders are the equivalent of the Guardians of the Galaxy for the team. They are equal parts mentor, guide, parent, coach, manager, leader, and visionary. Level four leaders are the glue that binds the group together—setting the culture, inspiring the team, and keeping the trains running on time.

When you become a level four leader, you have a job comparable to the CEO of a multimillion-dollar company. You're making monumental decisions that are impacting tens of thousands of people. But when you enroll Jessie tomorrow—she needs you to interact with her just like you are her normal sponsor. Because that's what you are.

The actions you must take to qualify at each level are worth some serious contemplation. Be honest and evaluate what level you're really at and what you need to change in order to reach the next level. Because the single most important thing you will ever do to create a leadership factory in your team—is to be continually evolving as a better leader yourself.

This business doesn't need more managers. We have plenty of those already.

Managers help people to see themselves as they are. And that is sometimes necessary.

But leaders help people to see who they can become. Which is why we need you to become a leader!

CHAPTER 17

Becoming Wealthy, Not Just "Instagram Rich"

Ever see those movies where some poor urchin from the street becomes wealthy and doesn't know how to act? (Like when Richard Gere took Julia Roberts to that fancy restaurant in *Pretty Woman*?) It's a timeless trope in Hollywood, guaranteed for good laughs.

That was me.

There's even a catchy name for it: nouveau riche. (The English equivalent is "new rich" or "new money.") It's a derogatory term to describe those upstart people whose wealth has been acquired within their own generation, rather than inheriting it from their rich, prominent, and illustrious family.

I'm nouveau riche. Or, as I preferred to be called, "white trash with cash." 😄 Some people whose families have generations of wealth look down on the newly rich. They seem to believe there is more honor in having your parents give you wealth instead of earning it yourself. How weird is that?

One of the terrific aspects about our profession is how many people are able to create wealth for themselves and their loved ones. But that does bring a few challenges.

The first of these is helping these newly wealthy people deal with the changes and responsibilities that come with wealth. For years I've been contemplating writing a book titled *What to Do When You Get Money*. Seriously.

When you start out poor and become rich, everything changes. The number of weddings, birthdays, and bar mitzvahs you're invited to increases exponentially. (You can expect invitations from the cable installer to the bag boy at your supermarket.)

Now that you have some real cash, you have to actually think about things like taxes, investments, and succession planning. And you have friends, family, and entourages that come to you every time they need a loan, wish to start a business, or want to set up a charitable foundation to run a home for unwed llamas.

In Direct Selling, we are often taking blue-collar employees on a modest income and putting them into a situation where they're now extremely high-paid entrepreneurs. An overwhelming majority of these people are simply not prepared for this.

So about 15 years ago, I began to offer some training for my higher level of leaders on the topics of selling the dream, investing to grow your business, and how to manage money. I'd like to share some of that training with you here.

Important Note: I am not a financial planner, accountant, investment advisor, or tax expert. I have no certification in any of these fields. To obtain advice and guidance in those areas, you should engage a qualified professional.

Remember, I'm just white trash with cash. But I have earned *a lot of cash*. Probably more than most of the people you know with the certifications above. And I have some very beneficial experience on how the way you manage and utilize your money can influence the activity and results of your team. So please take the advice I'm giving in this chapter within that context, and that context alone. (And to those of you who are company executives and top earners—think about how you can integrate this kind of training in the leadership retreats and award trips for your people at the higher ranks.)

THE HIERARCHY OF SELLING THE DREAM

It's almost a corny trope in our business that it's necessary to "sell the dream." But don't discount the necessity of this. People are being beaten down and programmed with negative and limiting beliefs on a continuous basis. Many do forget about or even give up on their dreams. We need to help them bring those dreams back to life.

However, make sure you're doing this with integrity and in a way that actually moves your team forward, not backward. You need to be mindful about what culture you're creating.

People share their "risen from the ashes" stories to inspire others. They're posting photos of their bonus car, their free trip to that swanky beach resort, and the jewelry they purchased that would make a rapper blush.

Others on their team want to emulate them. They believe the secret is "fake it 'til you make it," and they start staging photo shoots. There are people who rent a sports car for a day, then create social media posts and profiles as though they own it. They're somehow under the impression that these garish updates will inspire candidates to join or that all their team members will work harder. Then, the logic goes, they will actually be able to afford this "Instagram rich" mirage of a lifestyle.

The last time this actually worked successfully was never.

Here's another type of trap to avoid. Let's say your income is now up to $25,000 a month. You see a swanky-looking wristwatch for $25K. You tell yourself, "I should buy this now. When my team sees I can afford something like that, they'll be so inspired to work harder that the watch will pay for itself. And it's only one month's income anyway."

Um…no.

First of all, that's not one month's income, that's one month's gross revenue. From that $25,000 you have to take out taxes, which might be anywhere from $7,000 to $10,000. Then what about the airline tickets and hotel rooms you paid for that month? And the other marketing materials and other expenses?

So that watch might actually require three or four months' worth of earnings. And the probability that this particular piece of jewelry will inspire such a dramatic and immediate increase in volume so as to pay for itself is a fraction of a percentage so small it would require a microscope to see it.

I have no problem with you buying expensive watches. (I'm a watch addict, with more than 200 of them.) But buy them when you can afford them, pay cash for them, and because you enjoy them— not with the foolish belief they are going to grow your team.

Often people in our business rent or purchase a bigger home than they can afford, also thinking this will impress and inspire their team members. In reality, very few people from your team will ever see your home. What most people will notice first will be your clothing and jewelry. (Because they see you at events so often.)

A lot of people think that buying or leasing an upscale car or upmarket home will generate a bunch of new distributors for them. That doesn't really happen. So please make sure the culture on your team doesn't embolden imprudent financial decisions.

The best culture to set is one where emerging leaders counsel with the proven leaders above them before making any significant financial and lifestyle decisions. There is a hierarchy of making these lifestyle changes as your business grows. The one I follow and recommend is this:

- Clothes
- Jewelry
- Car
- First class travel
- Home
- Flying private, buying yachts, etc.

In the usual scenario, once someone starts to earn some serious money, they will need to upgrade their wardrobe and image. As we discussed earlier, many people we bring into the business have no experience in fashion or business attire. That's okay, as we all have to start somewhere.

As men become more successful, they will need to trade in their off-the-rack suit that was never altered to fit them properly for one that is. Later on, they'll probably evolve to bespoke suits. Some women will need to learn the distinction between a cocktail gown and a business dress. When leaders reach the highest ranks, they're going to be receiving awards on stage at galas, where tuxedoes and evening gowns are the appropriate attire. Some of them will need advice from the sponsorship line on when and where to buy these items.

After that, they may want to buy some nice jewelry. If your company has a bonus car program, the car decision will be predicated upon that. If you don't have a car program, counsel with your people so they aren't getting on the hook for car payments they can't afford. It will be better if they keep growing their business while setting aside enough money so they can purchase their next auto with cash.

Likewise, counsel with them as they proceed up the hierarchy of selling the dream. Encourage them to first pay off their credit cards and work to become debt-free. As the business and their income get bigger, they can alter their lifestyle accordingly.

You'll have much more success if you promote a culture of debt-free living than you ever will by encouraging people to act Instagram rich and hope the hype will entice candidates. Help your people invest wisely and make prudent upgrades in their lifestyle. You and they should be building for the future.

If you desire grand homes with 10-car garages, private jets, and enough bling-bling to make your heart sing-sing, I have no issue with you. But if you can't pay cash for it, don't do it.

I've made millions of dollars. But I promise, *you will never feel richer than the day you pay off your last credit card and become debt-free.*

The other culture so important in this area is that of investing in your business. Many people want to quit their job and live out of the business. That's a great goal. But too many people attempt it too early. The reason "selling the dream" works is because you see people actually moving up the economic ladder. You watch their lifestyle improve.

So let's say a woman makes $50,000 a year in her profession. She has credit card debt, student loans, a car payment, and a mortgage. She joins your team and works her income up to match the $50,000 she currently earns, so she quits.

She hasn't changed her lifestyle in any meaningful way. She's still someone who earns $50,000 a year, with credit card debt, student loans, a car payment, and a mortgage. She can work from home now and that's an improvement. But her financial security hasn't improved.

Better you create a culture where she continues to increase the time devoted to her business while keeping her job. She reinvests all of her business profits back into the business or paying down her debt. Then when she's debt-free and quits her job, both her standard of living *and* financial security have improved.

One of the frequent landmines for new people who reach success in our business is taxes. They're used to having their taxes automatically deducted from their paycheck. Then when they become an entrepreneur, they don't make deposits or set aside the money for taxes every month. (I wouldn't know anything about this. 😩) This can snowball quickly and cause extreme pressure. So educate your team early on to avoid this scenario.

Start by reinvesting everything back into the business when you begin. Your percentage of business expenses should go down as your check goes up. To build wealth, a sensible strategy is to increase your savings percentage as the amount of your check rises. Table 17.1 is an example of what this can look like at different income levels.

Table 17.1 Budgeting Your Bonus Check

Example 1

Item	Amount	%
Bonus Check	$ 10,000	—
Business Expense	2,500	—
Net	7,500	100
Tithe	750	10
Taxes	2,625	35
Savings	750	10
Live On	$ **3,375**	**45**

Example 2

Item	Amount	%
Bonus Check	$ 40,000	—
Business Expense	10,000	—
Net	30,000	100
Tithe	3,000	10
Taxes	10,500	35
Savings	4,500	15
Live On	$ **12,000**	**40**

Example 3

Item	Amount	%
Bonus Check	$ 100,000	—
Business Expense	15,000	—
Net	85,000	100
Tithe	8,500	10
Taxes	29,750	35
Savings	17,000	20
Live On	$ **29,750**	**35**

You might think that it would be impossible to earn $40,000 or $50,000 a month and end up in financial trouble. But I can assure you—not only is that possible, it happens far too often in our business. Include developing financial literacy in your training agendas and culture, and your team will have a much greater chance for true financial security.

Next... we're going to bring this all home with the brutal truth that nobody else will tell you!

CHAPTER 18

The Brutal Truth Nobody Else Will Tell You...

8 p.m. The telephone rang. (No, it wasn't a ping from my cell phone. It was the telephone mounted on my wall, with the 15-foot cord between the handle and the base. You can Google it. 😊) It was Jim, my partner in a struggling business.

"Hey, what are you doing this Saturday afternoon?" he asked.

"Think I'm free. Why? What's up?"

"I might need you to protect me..."

Not knowing Jim to be the needy type, I said, "Protect you? From what?"

"Well, I was at a gas station filling up my car today, and the guy on the other side of the pump started talking to me about making money. He's coming over to show me something. I want you there to protect me, because I think it's Amway."

"Amway? What's Amway?" I wanted to know.

"You don't know what Amway is? It's that thing where they draw all those circles about making money."

"Jimmy, I don't know anything about circles or Amway. But if it's about making money—we need to make some money!"

That fateful Saturday arrived. The guy sat across from us at Jimmy's kitchen table, reached into his briefcase, and produced a yellow notepad along with a red pen. He drew a circle at the top of the page, and in that circle, he wrote "you."

Under that circle, he drew five more. And under those, 25 more. And then 125 more. And then…

I started hallucinating. As a high school dropout with limited educational background, I'd never been exposed to the concept of leverage before. I heard Elvis singing *Blue Suede Shoes*.

I signed up, on the spot. And while I did not end up staying with Amway, it is certainly a fine company that has helped a great many people. And since it's taking down about $8 billion a year, they seem to have been able to eke out an existence without me.

I had no way of knowing it then, but that decision to join Direct Selling, at 20 years old, would transform my life forever.

I've earned millions of dollars in commissions, a fleet of exotic supercars, lived in beautiful homes around the globe, and traveled to more than 70 countries. And those are the least important benefits I received…

The business introduced me to the concept of personal development. (A concept I didn't even know existed.) Thus began a lifelong journey that has, thus far, transformed a young, neurotic, naïve, insecure person with social anxiety—into a confident, poised individual with healthy self-esteem.

And brought me the greatest benefit: relationships I treasure with extraordinary people.

If I could write a letter to that naïve 20-year-old self, here's what I would tell him…

Dear Young Randy,

As you embark on this new journey in your life, there are some things I want you to know. I've traveled back in time, because these lessons are so important to your future success and happiness. They're the lessons you're going to learn over the next four decades. Allow me to reveal them to you now...

When you host your first meeting, no one is going to show up.

I know that you've already done the calls and have 17 people who have confirmed to come. None of them are going to actually show up. Not one.

But you will make a choice that evening. You will decide between dropping out or giving your future a better chance. You will search your soul and come to a fascinating revelation. You will realize that you are the most ambitious person you know. And that will create the foundation for all of your later success in life.

You're going to have a terrible sponsor.

Over the course of your decades in the business, you'll have a number of sponsors. But the one who impacts your future the most will be the terrible one. Please know that having a weak sponsor will make you stronger. And that won't happen any other way.

Invest in fixing your teeth sooner.

It's going to take corrective surgery, removing a tooth, and wearing braces. (Three times.) But having bad teeth is a real disability. Because that situation makes

(continued)

you afraid to smile. And a smile is the most effective recruiting tool that has ever been invented. So make the investment in your teeth sooner. Most dentists have financing options.

Whenever you're in doubt and not sure which way to turn, take action.

Action defeats procrastination. Action lowers stress. Action cures doubt. Action conquers fear.

No one from your immediate family is going to join your business.

Okay, a few will enroll to pander to you, but they're going to drop out soon after. And that's okay.

Sometimes you are the "hometown prophet" and those closest to you cannot release the old, established perception they have of you.

Just be you. A lot sooner.

Right now, people are telling you that the only route to success means wearing a blue suit, white shirt, and red tie. And you'll repeat that advice to others, because you don't know any better.

Don't be so quick to buy into conventional wisdom about what is professional, appropriate, or normal. Respect it, think about it, but don't accept it blindly. The only way you can ever become a great leader of people and change the trajectory of the universe is to be your absolute, true, and authentic self. The people who don't accept you are not your tribe, and you shouldn't spend even two seconds worrying about that.

Insulting people is not a very effective recruiting strategy.

When you're new to the business, you have a certainty that you and your company are the greatest in the world. And that every other opportunity must be inferior. But explaining to people why they are stupid to be in a different [company, comp plan, product line, sponsorship line] than yours won't produce the results you think they will.

Stop beating yourself up so hard.

The opposite of success is not failure. The opposite of success is mediocrity. Failure, obstacles, and making mistakes are an integral part of the journey toward success. Let your mantra be this:

My vices are the property of my learning, my virtues belong to truth, my wisdom comes from my mistakes, and my challenges create my victories.

Learn the importance of your vision sooner.

Oh, you'll figure this out along the way. But speed up the process. Because the state you ultimately want to reach is self-mastery.

But self-mastery, like mastery of all kinds, means excelling above most others, achieving the highest levels of effort, practice, and execution. Being willing to sacrifice to be the best. And once you attain this kind of mastery, the business transforms from difficult and arduous to pleasurable and almost effortless. So let me share how you get there. Zeroing in on the very essence, the formula for self-mastery is extremely simple, yet remarkably profound.

(continued)

Mastery comes from confidence. Confidence comes from achieving goals. Achieving goals comes from daily habits. Your daily habits are created by the vision you hold.

Once you've done the dream building and really own the vision of who you desire to become, your daily habits will get you there. Which takes us to the next item on my list…

Dream bigger.

Because if your dreams are not bold, daring, and a little frightening—why bother with them at all?

Integrity will serve you well.

Later in life, you will meet an extremely short, but exceedingly wise green man. He will advise you, "If you choose the quick and easy path as Vader did—you will become an agent of evil." That advice will serve you the rest of your days.

Companies are going to offer you secret, under-the-table deals. One time they will show up with a briefcase containing $100,000 cash and offer to leave it behind for an endorsement for them. You'll refuse these offers, even though you could really use that money at the time. But you will be so glad you acted the way you did. Your integrity will become the most powerful recruiting tool you'll ever have.

Your freedom is on the other side of your fear.

The candidates you have the most fear of calling are usually the best ones. The work that seems to be the most intimidating often provides the greatest satisfaction. And the goal that seems the most daunting is actually the one that pulls you toward it.

Know that you will make a real difference.

Yes, you will walk across the stage to adulation, earn a fortune, and make a name for yourself. You will become successful. And also know that eventually you will move from success to something much more priceless: Significance.

Think about the collateral impact our business has for people. How many relationships were strengthened or saved because spouses came together to work toward a common goal? How many mothers (and fathers) got to go back home and raise their own kids, instead of paying someone else to do it?

How many millions of people—who have never even been a distributor—have had their lives enhanced because of products supplied by a Direct Selling company? What about the pounds lost, the nutritional deficiencies alleviated, the energy restored, or maybe just the money saved on the monthly phone bill or other utilities that was put to better use?

How many more people support charities because of the money and freedom they've earned from the business? A future president, the doctor who finds a cure for disease, or the person who creates the starship that can take us to Jupiter may be the person who got a college education on the money their parents are earning today in Leveraged Sales.

Yes, there are tens of thousands of people who are in the business but will never get wealthy. Be okay with

(continued)

that. Because the potential is there for them if they choose it. Most people will benefit from the products; some will benefit from the personal growth; and the serious ones will become wealthy.

So what you are doing will make a difference. Never lose sight of that.

Sincerely,

Your Future You

Of course we both know I can never go back and share these things with the younger me. But I can share them with you.

So I just did.

RECOMMENDED RESOURCES

Training and other resources from Randy:

www.randygage.com

https://leveragedsales.com

Mastermind Event: https://www.mastermindevent.com

Moo Cards: https://www.moo.com/us

Randy's Leadership Academy: www.gagevt.com

Power Prosperity Podcast: https://anchor.fm/powerprosperity

"DID THIS GUY WRITE ANYTHING ELSE?"

How to Build a Multi-Level Money Machine

Accept Your Abundance

37 Secrets About Prosperity

Prosperity Mind

101 Keys to Your Prosperity

The 7 Spiritual Laws of Prosperity

Why You're Dumb, Sick, and Broke and How to Get Smart, Healthy, and Rich!

Risky Is the New Safe

Mad Genius

Lead Your Team!

Coming February 2020:

DEFCON 1 Leadership

ACKNOWLEDGMENTS

Whether you know it or not, you have been greatly blessed by the people in my life. The book you have just read has been made immeasurably better because of a team of dedicated professionals (who happen to also be wonderful people) whom I turn to for advice. They generously offered their time, brilliance, and empathy—to help create a resource that will help you and millions of other people around the world move closer to their dreams.

I want to express my deep, heartfelt gratitude to this group of superstars. Every person listed in the front who provided a quote about the book also read chapter proofs and provided extremely valuable guidance for how to make the book more helpful for you. Editor Vicki McCown, whom I pay to be mean to me. And the dedicated team at Wiley who pays me to let them be mean to me: Matt Holt, Zach Schisgal, Vicki Adang, Peter Knox, Shannon Vargo, and the team at Cape Cod Compositors. Last, but certainly not least, Bob Erdmann who spreads my work in languages around the globe.

May the Force be with you all!

ABOUT THE AUTHOR

If you want to reach success in Leveraged Sales, there is probably no one on earth better qualified to help you than **Randy Gage**. An icon of the profession, Randy helped introduce Direct Selling in many developing countries and has trained the top income earners in dozens of companies. He has arguably trained more million-dollar producers than anyone alive today.

Most importantly, Randy teaches from real-world experience, having earned millions of dollars as a distributor and built a team of more than 200,000 people. In 2014, Randy was the first person inducted into the Direct Selling Hall of Fame.

Randy is the author of 11 books translated into 25 languages, including the *New York Times* bestsellers *Risky Is the New Safe* and *Mad Genius*. He has spoken to more than two million people across more than 50 countries and has also been inducted into the CPAE Speaker Hall of Fame. When he is not prowling the platform or locked in his lonely writer's garret, you'll probably find him playing third base for a softball team somewhere.

INDEX

A

Academy for Network Marketing
    Leadership, 13
Accountability, 204–205
Action, taking, 260
Active lines, 240
Administrative managers, 45
Alibaba, 143
Almaty, Kazakhstan, 3
Amazon, 93–94
Amway, 93, 143, 257–258
Apple, 189–191
Arbonne, 93
Archimedes, 1
Assignments, 206–207
Attitude, 220
Autoship, 66
Avon, 144

B

Back office, 66
"Bait and switch," 18–19
Basic inventory, 91–92
Behavior, 220
Belief, 220
Binary compensation plans, 49–51
Bios, 195–196
Blockbuster Video, 43

Blockchains, 16, 22
Branded resellers, 150
Break-even point, 161
Buffet, Jimmy, 191
Building lines, 155–158
Business-building time, 69–70
Business-building tools, 70
Business credit, 67
"Buyers" clubs, 30

C

Candidate lists, 70–72, 105
Candidates, xiv, 47–48
Capital, 43–45
Career paths, 58–60
Carnegie, Andrew, 1
Cash, 43–45
Casual builders, 235
CEOs, 45
Challenging, 208, 233
Chief financial officers, 45
Chief operations officer, 45
Chief technology officer, 45
China, 143
Choosing the right company, 25–62
    based on competency, 61
    choosing the right startup vs., 42–43
    debt, cash, capital, and, 43–45

Choosing the right company *(continued)*
  evaluating compensation plans and, 48–61
  illegal pyramids vs. legitimate pay plans and, 25–29
  management depth and, 45–46
  products and, 31–40
  questionable clubs and, 29–30
  sponsorship and, 40–42
  support structures and, 46–48
Cirque du Soleil, 190, 191, 245
Closing people, 80–81
Clubs, 29–30
Codes of Ethics, 67
College degrees, 4, 5, 21
Collins, Dana, 99
Commitment, 200, 223–225
Communicating, 145
Company policies, 67
Compensation plans, 48–61
  and balancing pay across levels, 55–57
  binary, 49–51
  and career paths, 58–60
  difference made by small amounts in, 57–58
  essentials for, 54–55
  and lifestyle rewards, 60–61
  well-designed, 51–54
Competency, 61
Conflicts, 207–208
"Con man (woman)," 185–186
Consistency, 223
Consumers, 26, 32
Cook, Tim, 189
"Cooked legs," 20
Core messages, 201–202
Counseling, 238–240
Critical mass, 45
Critical thinking, 7

Cryptocurrencies, 13, 16, 33–36
Customers, 13, 235, 239
Customer service managers, 45
Customer volume (CV), 13, 87–95, 239
  building, 90–94
  and leverage, 94–95
  scope of, 87–90

D
Debit cards, 67
Debt, 21, 43–45
Demonstrations, 92–93
DeVos, Doug, 143
Discernment, 18, 19
Distribution center managers, 45
Distributors:
  and compensation plans, 49, 52
  desirable qualities of, 39
  having 100 or more, 219
  as product consumers, 26–29
  and recruitment, 158
  and social media, 141
DōTERRA, 93
Dreamers, 7
Dress, 215
"Driven" lines, 77, 155–158
Duli, Andi, 64–65, 194
Duplication, 75–85, 153–161
  building lines vs. driving lines for, 155–158
  delineating, 81–84
  functionality vs., 76–77
  and leading by example, 160
  maintaining high retention for, 161
  and opening people vs. closing people, 80–81
  with people, 77
  securing lines for, 158–160
  and studying/doing/teaching, 79
  three-part formula for, 77–78

tools for, 79–80, 84
valid samples for, 78–79

E
EBay, 94
E-commerce, 46, 139–151
    embracing, 140–145
    and functionality/processes,
        144–145
    and potentially growing markets,
        143–144
    scope of, 139–140
Emotional connections, 38–40
Enrolling, 136–138, 145, 239
ESPN, 231
Ethics, 98–100
Events, 67–68, 217–220, 241–243
Exclusion, 201
Experience, 4–5
ExxonMobil, 62, 154

F
Facebook:
    building volume with, 145–146
    conducting home meetings vs., 122
    connecting to your sponsorship line
        with, 67
    how distributors use, 149–150
FaceTime, 169
Facilitation, 206
Failure, learning from, 261
Family members, 260
Fear, and freedom, 262–263
Field generals, 235
Financial security, 206
Focus:
    of direct selling business, xiv
    maintaining, 200
Fogg, John Milton, 93
Followers, casual builders as, 235

Freedom:
    cost of, xvii
    and fear, 262–263
"Front-loading," 26
Functionality, 76–77, 144–145

G
Gagevt.com, 70
Game plans, 202
Gamio, Erick, 194
Gates, Bill, 1
Getty, J. Paul, 1
"Gifting" clubs, 29
Godin, Seth, 191
"Greater fool theory," 35
Group dynamics, 202–203
Growth, 63–74
    with autoship, 66
    booking yourself for major events for,
        67–68
    building foundation for, 65–73
    and candidate lists, 70–72
    committing to, 64–65
    goals for, 68–69
    harnessing social media and e-com-
        merce to increase, *see* E-com-
        merce; Social media
    international, *see* International
        growth
    and "Major Blast," 73–74
    mindsets for, 63–64
    and ordering, 65–66
    scheduling for, 69–70
    tools for, 70
Gullibility, 18

H
Hard work, 7–8
Headhunters, 27
Head shots, 194

"Helicopter sponsors," 184
Herbalife, 13, 93
Home meetings, 122–125
"Hometown prophets," 182–183
Hotels, 127–128
How to Build a Multi-Level Money Machine (Gage), xvi, 48, 79

I
ICOs (initial coin offerings), 35–36
Image, 213–217
Impact, making, 263–264
Inclusion, 200–201
Income, 215
India, 143
Information funnels, 149
Initial coin offerings (ICOs), 35–36
Initial public offering (IPO), 35
Inspiring, 197–199
Instagram, 97, 139, 144, 150–151, 187
Integrity, 205, 262
Intensity, 202
International growth, 163–171
    long-distance lines as, 164–167
    starting new lines for, 168–171
Inventory repurchase, 28–29
Investing, in leaders, 232–233
Investments, in direct selling, 211
Invitations, 105–113
IPO (initial public offering), 35
Iroquois Indians, 77
Isagenix, 93

J
Jonak, Art, 13, 62, 139, 141

K
Knowledge, 220
Kodak, 43

L
"Ladder of escelation," 83, 84
La Paz, Bolivia, 3
Large-venue presentations, 127–132
Leaders, 8–9, 173–186, 197–208
    "BFFs" as, 181
    "blind, hungry dogs in a butcher shop" as, 181–182
    brands of, *see* Leadership brand
    "con man (woman)" as, 185–186
    by example, 160
    factories of, *see* Leadership factories
    "followers" as, 177–178
    great, 199–208
    "helicopter sponsors" as, 184
    "Hollywood directors" as, 185
    "hometown prophets" as, 182–183
    inspiring as, 197–199
    levels of, 245–248
    "mad geniuses" as, 176–177
    management of conflicts by, 207–208
    "martyrs" as, 173–174
    "messiahs" as, 175–176
    "moths" as, 178
    "ostriches" as, 178–179
    "party animals" as, 180
    "prince(ess) of darkness" as, 179
    "renegades" as, 182
    "sales pros" as, 180–181
    "shrewd investors" as, 183–184
    "social (media) butterflies" as, 176
    "tacticians" as, 174–175
Leadership brand, 187–196
    dynamics of, 188–189
    how to establish, 189–191
    positioning your own, 191–196
Leadership factories, 229–248
    foundations of, 233–236
    importance of, 229–231

investing in, 232–233
  and levels of leadership, 245–248
  in leveraged sales, 236–245
  teaching others how to think in,
    231–232
Leadership Institutes, 3
Leadership tracks, 243–244
Lead Your Team (Gage), 236
Legitimate pay plans, 25–29
Lehman Brothers, 43
Levels of leadership, 245–248
Leverage, 1, 6, 133
Leveraged Sales:
  best products for, 189
  cash flow problems in, 43–44
  and commitment, 225
  consistency in, 223
  customer-driven, 140, 141, 143
  difficulties of, 221
  and duplication, 80, 119
  experience in, 46
  finding business in, 87
  importance of, 57
  leaders in, 207, 232, 234
  and multi-level marketing, 15–18
  learning new skills for, 64
  and leverage, 94–95
  multi-level marketing vs., 15–18
  positives of, 211, 212
  and "renegades," 182
  scope of, 6, 22
  and social media, 145
  why people fail in, 159
Lifestyle photos, 194
Lifestyle rewards, 60–61, 133, 211
Lines:
  active, 240
  building, 155–158
  "driven," 77, 155–158
  long-distance, 164–167

  personal, 240
  securing, 158–160
  sponsorship, 67
  starting new, 168–171
Ljubljana, Slovenia, 3
London, England, 3
Long-distance lines, 164–167
Lyft, 115

M
Ma, Jack, 143
"Mad geniuses," 176–177
"Major Blasts":
  definition of, 73–74
  inviting people to launch meetings
    as, 106
  key elements of, 121
  in new markets, 169, 170
  and recruitment, 119
  and retailers, 135–136
  successful, 111
Making the First Circle Work (Gage), 209
Management, 45–46
Manufacturing, 44
Marketing, 145
Marketing vice presidents, 45, 46
"Martyrs," 173–174
Mary Kay, 93
Mass-market presentation tools, 84
Mastermind Event, 13, 207
The Matrix (film), 7
McDonald's, 81
Meeting new people, 102–104
Melloni, Luca, 133
Memphis, Tennessee, 3
Metrics, 239–240
Mistakes, 240–241
MLM, see Multi-level marketing
"MLM Zombies," 19, 61, 244
Money games, 13, 17, 48

MOO Cards, 116
Moscow, Russia, 3
Motivation, 63
Multi-level marketing (MLM), 9, 11–23,
    139, 143
    death of, 14–15
    and gullibility, 18
    and Leveraged Sales, 15–18
    not competing with, 19–20
    and not promoting large incomes,
        20–21
    protecting yourself/your team from,
        18–19
    scope of, 11–14
    and shaming, 21–23
Musk, Elon, 1

N
Nature's Sunshine, 93
Netflix, 8, 99
Network Marketing, *see* Multi-level
    marketing
Neuro-Linguistic Programming tech-
    niques (NLP), 80, 154, 243
New money, 249
Newton's Laws, 153
Nike, 190, 191
NLP (Neuro-Linguistic Programming
    techniques), 80, 154, 243
Nouveau riche, 249
Nu Skin, 93

O
One-on-one presentations, 126–127
Online presentations, 132–135, 147–148
Online presentation tools, 84
Online product trial offers, 149
Online sample offers, 148–149
Opening people, 80–81
Opportunity meetings, 148
Ordering, 65–66, 145

P
Passive income, 211
PBRs (Private Business Receptions),
    122–125
Pensacola, Florida, 3
Personal brand, 215
Personal development, 221–223
Personal lines, 240
Personal volume, 239
Physical presentation tools, 84
Pinterest, 143
Pizza Hut, 40
Policies and Procedures, 67
Ponzi schemes, 3, 13, 48
Positive leadership, 199
Posture, 72, 210–213
Potentially growing markets, 143–144
Power Prosperity Podcast, 222
Prerecorded streaming presentations, 148
Presentations, 136–138
Presentation tools, 84
Presidents, 45
"Prince(ess) of darkness," 179
Private Business Receptions (PBRs),
    122–125
Processes, 144–145
Product benefit-centered groups,
    149–150
Productivity, 205
Products, 31–40, 220
Product volume (PV), 13
Profiles, 146–147
Profit, 211
Prospecting talent, 97–118, 145
    candidate lists for, 105
    importance of ethics for, 98–100
    invitations in, 105–117
    and meeting new people, 102–104
Prosperity tables, 129
PR platforms, 19
Punctuality, 61

PV (product volume), 13
Pyramid schemes, 13, 17, 25–29, 48, 166

Q
Qualifying volume (QV), 13
Quantified ladders of escalation, 84

R
Radio Margaritaville, 191
"Rainmaker" activities, 225
Rank, 215, 239
Rank advancement, 205
Recognition, 202
Recruitment, 119–138, 205, 234
  conducting home meetings for, 122–125
  conducting online presentations, 132–135
  large-venue presentations for, 127–132
  negative tactics for, 261
  and retailers, 135–136
  scope of, 119–121
Regulation, xvi, 25, 26
"Renegades," 182
Repeatable results, 120
Residual income, 54–55, 211
Retailers, 135–136, 235
Retention, 161
Risky Is the New Safe (Gage), 189
Robbins, Sarah, 194
Robbins, Tony, 154
Rockefeller, John D., 1
Rodan + Fields, 93
Rosales, Lily, 133
"Running legs," 56

S
Sacrifice, 225–227
"Safe spaces," 77

"Sales pros," 180–181
San Diego, California, 3
Scheduling, 69–70
Securing lines, 158–160
Selling skills, 4, 6, 8
"Selling the dream," 251–256
SEO marketing (search engine optimization), 18
Seoul, South Korea, 3
Serious builders, 235
Shaming, 21–23
Shell, 62
Shopify, 94
"Shrewd investors," 183–184
Significant income, 57
Skillsets, 215, 220
Skopje, Macedonia, 3
Skype, 115, 126
Smiling, 259–260
Social media, 74, 139–151
  building volume with, 145–151
  direct selling changed by, xvi
  embracing, 140–145
  and functionality/processes, 144–145
  and potentially growing markets, 143–144
  scope of, 139–140
Social proof, 202–203
Speaking style, 215
Sponsorship, 40–42
Sponsorship lines, 67
Standardized new member orientation, 84
Standardized presentation outlines, 84
Starbucks, 190
Startup, 42–43
Stress, 211
Style, 215
Support structures, 46–48
Sydney, Australia, 3

T
Taiwan, 7
Tax breaks, 211
Teaching others how to think, 231–232
Teaching skills, 8
Teams, 209–227, 240
    building dream bigger than,
        199–200
    and commitment, 223–225
    and consistency, 223
    and events, 217–220
    and image, 213–217
    and personal development,
        221–223
    perspective of, 209–210
    and posture, 210–213
    and sacrifice, 225–227
Team volume, 239
Tickler files, 91
Toys "R" Us, 43
Training, 145
"Transfer buying," 66
Transitional income, 54–55
Travel, 211
Tribes (Godin), 191
Trujillo, Peru, 3
"Turnkey" businesses, 81
"Turn" questions, 90
Two-category coaching, 203–204

U
Uber, 37, 115, 116, 143, 230
United Kingdom, 57
United Nations, 98

United States, 57, 161
Users, *see* Consumers

V
Valid samples, 78–79
Vemma, 13
Viability, 36–38
Vision, importance of, 261–262
Volunteers, 233

W
Walton, Sam, 30
Wealth, 249–256
    and direct selling business participa-
        tion, xiii–xiv
    possessing, 249–250
    and "selling the dream," 251–256
WeChat, 149–150
Weekly leadership school, 133
WhatsApp, 67, 93, 139, 149–150
*Why You're Dumb, Sick, and Broke… and
    How to Get Smart, Healthy, and
    Rich!* (Gage), 222
Winfrey, Oprah, 1
Woolworth's, 43

Y
Yager, Dexter, 196
Young Living, 93
YouTube, 143

Z
Zagreb, Croatia, 3
ZOOM, 83, 115, 126, 165, 169